Lecture Notes in Computer Science   11398

Commenced Publication in 1973
Founding and Former Series Editors:
Gerhard Goos, Juris Hartmanis, and Jan van Leeuwen

More information about this series at http://www.springer.com/series/7410

Apostolos P. Fournaris
Konstantinos Lampropoulos
Eva Marín Tordera (Eds.)

Information and Operational Technology Security Systems

First International Workshop, IOSec 2018, CIPSEC Project
Heraklion, Crete, Greece, September 13, 2018
Revised Selected Papers

 Springer

Editors
Apostolos P. Fournaris
University of Patras
Patras, Greece

Konstantinos Lampropoulos
University of Patras
Patras, Greece

Eva Marín Tordera
Advanced Network Architectures Lab
Barcelona, Spain

ISSN 0302-9743   ISSN 1611-3349 (electronic)
Lecture Notes in Computer Science
ISBN 978-3-030-12084-9   ISBN 978-3-030-12085-6 (eBook)
https://doi.org/10.1007/978-3-030-12085-6

Library of Congress Control Number: 2018968327

LNCS Sublibrary: SL4 – Security and Cryptology

This Springer imprint is published by the registered company Springer Nature Switzerland AG
The registered company address is: Gewerbestrasse 11, 6330 Cham, Switzerland

Preface

In the modern era most companies, enterprises, public services etc. use the recent ICT (information and communication technology) advances to become more flexible, lower their operational costs, and promote their products and services. In terms of infrastructure, this evolution has introduced new types of networks, systems, and architectures, which in many cases derive from the interconnection of new and legacy technologies. Especially for industrial systems like critical infrastructures (CIs), which until recently mainly used operational technologies (OT; automation-based, control-based systems) the recent advances of ICT have given them the ability to offer new and innovative services, improve their management procedures, lower their maintenance costs, and create new business opportunities. However, this adaptation of new technologies was made rather quickly without proper evaluation of its impact on security, exposing these systems (industrial systems and CIs) to various new kinds of cyberattacks.

Industrial systems and CIs have very specific requirements (e.g., high responsiveness, real-time monitoring, specialized hardware, low computational capabilities etc.). These requirements make the process of integrating new technologies and components more complicated compared with other domains. In particular, the adaptation of new cybersecurity products may impose additional delays on the system's performance, power consumption, complexity etc. Such products may also require additional components, thus increasing the complexity of the overall system and its maintenance costs. On the other hand, the absence of cybersecurity countermeasures in sensitive systems like industrial systems or CIs can lead to devastating damage with significant impact on public safety and welfare. In view of these issues, the research community must further work on addressing the cybersecurity issues that emerge from the ongoing integration between IT and OT systems. There is a need to model IT/OT system assets, identify possible cybersecurity vulnerabilities, and provide prevention, detection, response, and mitigation security strategies/policies.

The International Workshop on Information & Operational Technology (IT & OT) Security Systems (IOSEC) aims to bring together viewpoints from diverse areas to explore the commonalities of security problems and solutions for advancing the collective science and practice of IT and OT security protection. In 2018, the workshop took place in September in collocation with the RAID 2018 conference and had input from various security research fields that can be applicable in the IT/OT security strengthening. The workshop lasted one full day, had 22 submitted papers, of which 12 were accepted, thus achieving an acceptance rate of $\sim 54\%$.

This book presents the research outcomes of the IOSEC 2018 Workshop by including extended versions of all the scientific works that were presented during the workshop. IOSEC 2018 was sponsored by the CIPSEC European Union Innovation action project "Enhancing Critical Infrastructure Protection with innovative Security framework" that develops a cybersecurity framework for critical infrastructure systems.

This framework, apart from technical security tools, is also introducing a wide set of cybersecurity services (vulnerability tests and recommendations, key personnel training courses, public–private partnerships [PPPs] forensics analysis, standardization, and protection against cascading effects) making the CIPSEC solution a complete security ecosystem for critical infrastructure protection.

This book is divided into three sections, each one focused on the cybersecurity research problems of specific IT/OT environments. Since the CI domain constitutes the best example of where the IT/OT ecosystems interconnect and cybersecurity failures have the highest impact on society and public welfare, the first section of this book is specifically dedicated to this domain. In this section, there are four chapters where authors discuss and propose solutions on: how to achieve unclonable identities of security designs (based on hardware), how to introduce efficient and secure access control mechanisms on file systems, how to protect the cloud level that may exist in various critical infrastructure systems by pointing to their vulnerabilities, and finally how to detect attacks on CAN messages (a typical communication protocol on OT systems) using heuristics and neural networks.

The second section is focused on more generic concepts of IT/OT cybersecurity including cybersecurity threat modeling, vulnerability assessment based on questionnaires, and techniques in order to address privacy issues of IT/OT systems employees social network identities and interests.

Finally, the third section of this book is dedicated to malware threats in IT/OT systems. Malicious software is a very important problem in such systems and recently it has found fertile ground in OT systems since the latter were not originally designed for security (but mostly for safety). The authors of this section propose solutions on how to detect software vulnerabilities that can be used by malware as well as solutions on how to detect malwares in IT and OT environments. More specifically, this section describes mechanisms for automatic patching application software after detecting possible exploitable vulnerabilities, clustering of malware based on called API during runtime, malware context searching mechanisms for specific malware collections, and finally a cloud-focused anti-malware engine using graphic processing unit accelerated network monitoring.

We would like to thank all the people who contributed to the realization of the IOSEC 2018 Workshop, the RAID Organizing Committee that took care of all the local arrangements, the IOSEC Program Committee and reviewers who helped us with the review process, and finally Springer for aiding us with the post-conference proceedings publication.

December 2018

Konstantinos Lampropoulos
Apostolos P. Fournaris
Eva Marín Tordera

Organization

General Chairs

Kostas Lampropoulos   University of Patras, Greece
Eva Marín Tordera   Universitat Politècnica de Catalunya, Spain

Publication and Publicity Chair

Apostolos P. Fournaris   University of Patras, Greece

Technical Program Committee

Antonio Álvarez   Atos, Spain
Rodrigo Díaz   Atos, Spain
Apostolos P. Fournaris   University of Patras, Greece
Odysseas Koufopavlou   University of Patras, Greece
Xavi Masip   Universitat Politècnica de Catalunya, Spain
Stefan Katzenbeisser   Technical University of Darmstadt, Germany
Neeraj Suri   Technical University of Darmstadt, Germany
Sotiris Ioannidis   Foundation for Research and Technology – Hellas, Greece
Christos Papachristos   Foundation for Research and Technology – Hellas, Greece
Vassilis Prevelakis   TU Braunschweig, Germany
Samuel Fricker   FHNW Fachhochschule Nordwestschweiz, Switzerland
Elias Athanasopoulos   University of Cyprus, Cyprus
Sharon Keidar-Barner   IBM Israel
Marco Spruit   Universiteit Utrecht, The Netherlands
Ciprian Oprisa   Bitdefender, Romania
Spyros Denazis   University of Patras, Greece
Dimitrios Serpanos   ISI/ATHENA, University of Patras, Greece
Nicolas Sklavos   University of Patras, Greece
Paris Kitsos   Technological Educational Institute of Western Greece

Sponsor

EU Horizon 2020 project CIPSEC
Enhancing Critical Infrastructure Protection with innovative
SECurity framework

Contents

Critical Infrastructure Cybersecurity Issues

A Cipher Class Based on Golden S-Boxes for Creating Clone-Resistant Identities

Saleh Mulhem$^{(\boxtimes)}$, Ayoub Mars, and Wael Adi

Institute of Computer and Network Engineering, TU Braunschweig,
38106 Braunschweig, Germany
s.mulhem@tu-bs.de

Abstract. Secret Unknown Cipher (SUC) concept was proposed as a promising technique to create clone-resistant electronic units as alternative to overcome the weaknesses of the traditional Physical Unclonable Functions (PUFs). A low-complexity real-field realization scenario for the proposed SUC concept is presented in this work. The key realization concept is making use of the so-called Golden S-Boxes as basic building blocks of block ciphers. According to the new proposed concept, the cipher creator called "GENIE" generates unknown ciphers with relatively low memory and time complexities. The target technology to accommodate the proposed self-created hard to predict SUCs is the non-volatile FPGA System on Chip (SoC) units converting them into clone-resistant entities.

Keywords: Secret Unknown Cipher · Physical Unclonable Function · Golden S-Boxes

1 Introduction

The demand for more efficient physically secure technologies is a permanent growing necessity. This is reflected by the emerging technological progress resulting in increasing security requirements. Recently these requirements have imposed on the technology systems some new criteria such as lightweight encryption/decryption, an efficient identification mechanism and low bandwidth message transfer [1]. In the last decade Physical Unclonable Functions (PUFs) were proposed and partially deployed to meet such requirements, especially in RFID, smart cards, mobile devices, wireless sensor networks and different applications of Internet of Things (IoTs) [2]. The core idea of PUF is making use of a physical entity that is embodied or naturally available in a physical or electronic structure. Moreover, PUF is defined as a random mapping which is easy to read and hard to reverse. At the same time, for any known inputs of PUF the outputs are very difficult or impossible to predict. Therefore, a PUF is mathematically modelled as a non-invertible one-way function. In particular, PUF works as an electronic-DNA, as every device is identified based on its physical characteristics, like DNA for human beings [4]. However, most PUFs have inconsistent behavior, because of aging effect and various environmental perturbations such as temperature and supply energy [2]. By making use of PUF's defects, Rührmair et al. [3] presented a modeling attack on PUFs. Where, a set of Challenge-Response Pairs

© Springer Nature Switzerland AG 2019
A. P. Fournaris et al. (Eds.): IOSec 2018, LNCS 11398, pp. 3–14, 2019.
https://doi.org/10.1007/978-3-030-12085-6_1

(CRPs) of a PUF is given to a designed algorithm which behaves indistinguishably from the original PUF on almost all CRPs.

Recently, Secret Unknown Cipher (SUC) was proposed as a new alternative for PUF in [4]. SUC is introduced based on randomly self-creation of unknown crypto-functions which are deployed as digital PUFs. The concept of SUCs is expected to makes low-complexity electronic devices attractive for a broad spectrum of future applications such as identification/authentication of connected devices in IoT environment.

2 Related Work

In [12], Wu et al. defined a Physical Unclonable Pseudo Random Permutation (PUPRP) as a block cipher deploying PUFs to generate the cipher key. A 64×64 PUPRP is presented based on Feistel structure with a substitution-permutation network (SPN) as an inner function. Instead of 4-bit S-Boxes in SPN, 4×4 PUFs were serving as substitution function. Unfortunately, every 4×4 PUFs need a Helper Data Algorithm (HDA) to attain a stable response for every round. Where, HDA is usually used to overcome the instability problem of PUFs.

The Hardware- Software Digital PUF (HW-SW DPUF) was first proposed in [9]. Where HW-SW DPUF is given as a cascade of functions which are randomly chosen from a large class of random cryptographic functions. The authors theoretically explained how a cascade of functions can be used to result with one cryptographic random cipher mapping.

An approach of PUPRP was presented in [5]. A delay PUF is utilized as a key generator for two different variants of a Boolean function. The resulting PUPRP needed a huge number of clock cycles in the implementation on FPGA and required an extra bandwidth for a decryption process. To resolve the bandwidth problem, Xu et al.'s proposed a digital bidirectional function (DBF) in [1], which consists of two Boolean functions, an original function and its inverse. Every communication needs to distribute one Boolean function of DBF to the sender and its inverse to the receiver, that increases the complexity of the communication over a network of more than two users. Unfortunately, DBF proposal omitted the delay PUF which guarantees unclonability of DPUFs.

The key idea of SUC tries to attain clone-resistant system, which largely overcomes at the same time the PUFs inconsistency drawbacks and vulnerabilities. In [13] Mars et al. proposed a digital clone-resistant function prototype as a Random Stream Cipher (RSC).

The paper is organized as follows: SUC concept is defined as a pseudo random block cipher. Moreover, Smart Cipher Designer/GENIE who creates SUC is described. Then, the expected memory complexity of GENIE is computed. Where different structures of SUCs are presented. Finally, the security level of SUC is bounded.

3 SUC as a Target Cipher and Its Designer/Creator

In this section, the SUC creation-process and some notes on the concept of a Smart Cipher Designer/GENIE are presented. Where, these concepts require non-volatile System on Chip (SoC) FPGAs to be realized such as SmartFusion®2 SoC FPGA by Microsemi. However, self-reconfiguration is an important requirement that is still not offered by nowadays non-volatile SoC FPGAs. Recently, non-volatile technology is used for long-term permanent structures allows creating irreversible hardware locks when needed. Microsemi SoC chips/units include a mature flash-based FPGA fabric with an ARM Cortex-M3 microcontroller in the same chip. Moreover, the programmable logic blocks in (SoC) FPGA can be interconnected by a hierarchy of reconfigurable flash-based switches. In particular, hieratical structure makes penetrating into the internal hardware architectures very difficult for invasive attacks. In the sense that to reach a secret an attacker would most probably destroy the secret itself before reading it.

3.1 A GENIE as Unpredictable SUC Generator

The key idea of the creation of SUC is based on triggering a non-repeatable single-event random process to create an unknown combined Hardware-Software (HW-SW) module, which is very hard to predict, and also embedded permanently in a SoC unit [4]. Suppose that a Trusted Authority (TA) injects into each SoC unit a smart GENIE software. A GENIE is an oriental imaginary creature from 1001-night stories which can realize any wishes when it come out after rubbing on "Aladin" magic lamp. After being loaded, the GENIE-software starts creating a permanent (non-volatile), unpredictable, pseudo random block cipher by using random bits from a True Random Generator (TRG) as shown in Fig. 1. Being created by the unpredictable TRG-bits, the resulting cipher is not known. The GENIE should be directly deleted after completing the cipher creation. Hence a particular random unknown selection of an operational cipher (SUC), from a large/huge class of possibilities, is created in the SoC unit/chip.

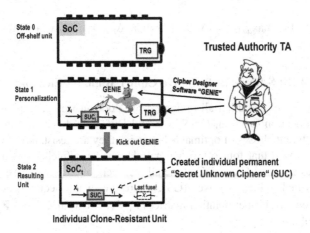

Fig. 1. Generating post-manufacturing physical identity.

The SUC module should be added to existing applications (devices) in the unused area on the SoC unit. Moreover, SoC units should be prohibited from being reconfigurable by setting some last-fuse hardware-lock as indicated in Fig. 1. The resulting SoC unit becomes physically unique as it is the only non-replaceable physical unit which can encrypt and decrypt by using the resulted unknown cipher. Generic unclonable identification protocols using such SUCs are presented in [14]. As the cipher is not known to anybody, the unit is basically hard to clone.

In the following sections, primitive security mappings and components, which a GENIE can use to generate SUCs at reasonable cost and complexity, are presented.

4   Cipher Design Strategy: Mappings and Preliminaries

In this section, the necessary design strategy for a SUC is presented. Where, a huge class of cryptographically-significant mappings is required to select one of them as a particular randomly elected SUC. Therefore, in perfect case, the cardinality of possible usable mappings should approach infinity. The smart cipher designer "GENIE" needs for optimal implementation simple and low-cost classes of mappings with good properties and high cardinality approaching infinity.

Let x denotes a vector $x = (x_{n-1}, \cdots, x_0)$ in $\mathbb{F}_2^n$ and let $F(x)$ denotes a Boolean function in n variables from $\mathbb{F}_2^n$ to $\mathbb{F}_2^n$.

A linearity of a Boolean function F is defined as follows,

$$Lin(F) = \max_{a,b \neq 0 \in \mathbb{F}_2^n} \left| F_b^W(a) \right| \tag{1}$$

Where, $F_b^W(a)$ is a Fourier coefficient at point (a, b) [6]. In this context, a Boolean function F is secure against Linear Cryptanalysis (LC) when its linearity is very small.

Let $\Delta_{F,a}^{-1}$ be a number of message pairs $(x, x + a)$ with the output difference b of a Boolean function F. The resistance of F against Differential Cryptanalysis (DC) is defined as follows,

$$Diff(F) = \max_{a \neq 0, b \in \mathbb{F}_2^n} \left| \Delta_{F,a}^{-1}(b) \right|, \text{ where } \Delta_{F,a}(x) = F(x) + F(x + a) \tag{2}$$

4.1   Golden 4-Bit S-Boxes as Primitive Cipher Building Elements

In [6], Leander et al. classified all optimal 4-bit Boolean functions (S-Boxes) which satisfy: S is a bijection function, $Lin(S) = 8$ and $Diff(S) = 4$. The results showed that there are 16 different classes of optimal S-boxes i.e. they are resistant to LC and DC. In [7], Saarinen showed that four of 16 optimal classes can affinely transform the resistance properties against LC and DC to the all members of classes. These optimal 4-bit S-Boxes are called golden S-Boxes (GS). Therefore, a new equivalence relation is defined based on two bit-permutation matrices P_i, P_k, two values $a, b \in \mathbb{F}_2^4$, and XOR-operation as follows,

$$[S(x)]_{1\times4} = GS_k\big([(x)]_{1\times4}\cdot[P_i]_{4\times4} \oplus [a]_{1\times4}\big)\cdot[P_k]_{4\times4} \oplus [b]_{1\times4} \qquad (3)$$

Where, GS_j is a golden S-Box for $k = 0, 1, 2, 3$ (See Table 1) and $x \in \mathbb{F}_2^4$.

In this proposal, a modification of (3) allows to create a subclass simply by more practical and efficient mapping implementation (see Fig. 2) as follows,

$$S(x) = [GS_k(x)]_{1\times4}\cdot[P_i]_{4\times4} \oplus [a]_{1\times4} \qquad (4)$$

Figure 2 shows the hardware sketch of two Golden S-Box generators according to (3) and (4). The resulting S-Boxes are cryptographically equivalent. Moreover, Golden S-Boxes are not only secure against LC and DC but also have the same algebraic properties such as branch numbers and circuit implementation complexity [7].

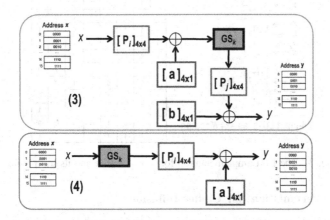

Fig. 2. Hardware sketch of the golden S-Box generators.

Table 1 shows four classes of the golden S-Boxes which satisfy the ideal properties for all members in the class. To store the set $G = \{GS_0, GS_1, GS_2, GS_3\}$ as a matrix of a truth tables (see Fig. 3), a memory of 512 Bits (128 bits $\times$ number of GSs) is required.

Table 1. The classes of the golden S-Boxes.

Canonical representative [7] 0123456789ABCDEF	Golden S-Box	# of possible GSs created by (3)	# of possible GSs created by (4)
035869C7DAE41FB2	GS_0	$147456 \approx 2^{17.1}$	$384 \approx 2^{8.5}$
03586CB79EADF214	GS_1	$147456 \approx 2^{17.1}$	$384 \approx 2^{8.5}$
03586AF4ED9217CB	GS_2	$147456 \approx 2^{17.1}$	$384 \approx 2^{8.5}$
03586CB7A49EF12D	GS_3	$147456 \approx 2^{17.1}$	$384 \approx 2^{8.5}$

It is very important to notice that only 19584 members from each class have a (single) cycle structure property [7].

4.2 Hardware Structure of the Used S-Boxes

Figure 3 shows that 4 4-input LUTs are required for implementing a 4×4 mapping. The 4×4 mapping $F = (y_0, y_1, y_2, y_3)$ can be seen as the parallel application of four Boolean functions $y_i = f_i(x_0, x_1, x_2, x_3)$, where $i = 0, 1, 2, 3$ (see Fig. 3). If f_i is non-linear for every i, then all 4×4 function F are called S-Boxes. The number of all possible 4-bit S-Boxes is equal to the number of all 4-input/4-output functions that is $2^{4 \cdot 2^4} = 2^{64}$. As a result, the implementation of any one golden S-Box requires 4 LUTs.

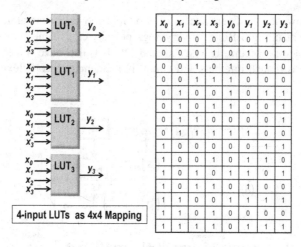

x_0	x_1	x_2	x_3	y_0	y_1	y_2	y_3
0	0	0	0	0	0	1	0
0	0	0	1	0	1	0	1
0	0	1	0	1	0	1	0
0	0	1	1	1	0	0	0
0	1	0	0	1	0	1	1
0	1	0	1	1	0	0	1
0	1	1	0	0	0	0	1
0	1	1	1	1	1	0	0
1	0	0	0	0	0	1	1
1	0	0	1	0	1	1	0
1	0	1	0	1	1	0	1
1	0	1	1	0	1	0	0
1	1	0	0	1	1	1	1
1	1	0	1	0	0	0	0
1	1	1	1	0	1	1	1

Fig. 3. The LUT implementation for 4×4 S-Box and its truth table.

4.3 Bundle Permutations for Cipher Diffusion

A Bundle Permutation (BP) is a permutation that changes the positions of the bundles without changing the positions of the bits within a bundle [8]. Figure 4 shows different (m, k)-BPs. Where, k is a number of the bundle's branches and m is a bit size of every branch. Recently, BPs are used in modern cipher like CAST-256, RC6 [10] and Khudra [11]. For example, Type-1, Type-2 and Type-3 Feistel networks [10] deploy the same PB as a permutation layer.

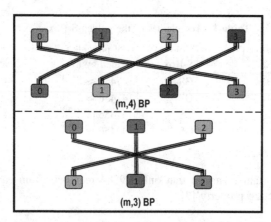

Fig. 4. Two examples of the bundle permutations.

For cryptographic security, the question remains how many iterations of BP the cipher needs to reach full diffusion. The cycle structure property of BP and its branch number are the most important factors to answer this question. Here an exhaustive search has been performed to test the cycle structure preparty of all (4, 4)-BPs and (4, 3)-BPs. An exhaustive search showed that 6 out of all (4, 4)-BPs and 2 out of all (4, 3)-BPs have the (single) cycle structure preparty (see Table 2).

Table 2. Two classes for the Bundle Permutations.

(4,4)-PBs	0	1	2	3
BP_0	1	2	3	0
BP_1	1	3	0	2
BP_2	2	0	3	1
BP_3	2	3	1	0
BP_4	3	0	1	2
BP_5	3	2	0	1
(4,3)-PBs	**0**	**1**	**2**	
BP_0	1	2	0	
BP_1	2	0	1	

Figure 5 shows the alternating PBs of Type-1, Type-2 and Type-3 with a single round $r = 1$. The information-theoretical optimal bounds are determined in [10] for Type-1, Type-2, and Type-3. The proof shows that an adversary needs at least $2^{n(1-\varepsilon)}$ queries to reach a good advantage for a successful attack.

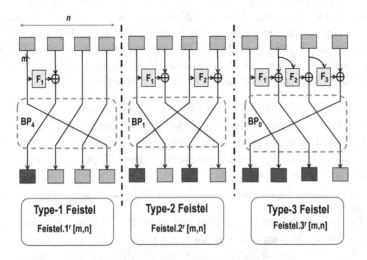

Fig. 5. Types for generalized Feistel networks.

5 SUC-Creating GENIE and Its Complexity

The SUC creation-process is performed by a GENIE (a software program) that will run in an initialization process for each unit. The GENIE should be simple and fast, as well as consume as small as possible of memory to be stored in temporarily. Therefore, the trade-off between a good performance and the required memory size should be carefully determined.

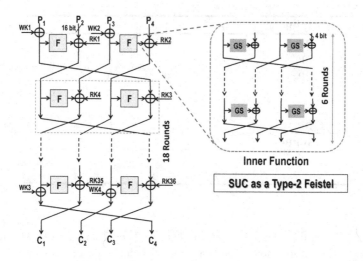

Fig. 6. A sample 64-bit SUC-cipher using type-2 Feistels with BP$_4$ bundle choice for the structure and inner function [11].

Assume that a GENIE deploys three different cipher schemes like Type-1, Type-2 and Type-3 Feistel networks. Here, a GENIE should select randomly one of the schemes as a cipher structure and also as an inner function F (see Fig. 6). In [11] Kolay et al. showed that using the Type-2 (with PB$_4$ and an optimal S-Box (see Fig. 6)) as a cipher structure and also as an inner function F makes the resulting cipher secure against LC and DC. The GENIE tasks can proceed as follows:

- GENIE selects randomly one of the PBs from $\{BP_i\}_{i=0}^{5}$ and
- GENIE selects randomly one of the golden S-Boxes from $\{GS_i\}_{i=0}^{3}$.
- GENIE uses (3) or (4) to generate randomly a sufficient number of golden S-Boxes
- GENIE selects randomly one of structures (Type-1, Type-2, and Type-3) which uses also for the inner function F.
- GENIE determines the number of rounds randomly $r \geq min$, (the minimum r will be given in Sect. 6).
- GENIE consumes 80 bits as a master key from the TRG for key scheduling part, which generates the round-keys as shown in [11].
- When the GENIE completes these tasks, the GENIE fully deletes itself.

Such operations can be performed on-the-fly at a very high-speed. Here, the GENIE requires relatively low hardware and software complexities. However, the resulting SUC has excellent properties to provide every SoC unit by a permanent and individual cipher as an electronic DNA identity randomly selected from $2^{232.9}$ possible cipher choices for the rest of its lifetime (see Sect. 5.1).

5.1 The GENIE's Complexity Figures

In this proposal, a possible design of GENIE requires 920 Bits to store 4 golden S-Boxes, 24 bit-permutation matrices, and 6 BPs. In addition, 128 bits need to be stored for every new golden S-Box.

Assume that the GENIE will use τ_i golden S-Boxes for the inner function F. Where, τ_i is determined based on minimum round r in Sect. 6. Here $\tau_1 = 1, \cdots 8$ if F is chosen as Type-1, $\tau_2 = 1, \cdots, 12$ if F is chosen as Type-2, and $\tau_3 = 1, \cdots 12$, if F is chosen as Type-3. Therefore, the total number of F choices is given as follows,

$$\mu = 4 \times \left(\binom{384}{\tau_1} + \binom{384}{\tau_2} + \binom{384}{\tau_3} \right) \times 6 \tag{5}$$

The μ count reaches a maximum for $\tau_1 = 8$, $\tau_2 = 12$ and, $\tau_3 = 12$. In this case, the GENIE generates a large number of SUCs,

$$\sigma = \sigma_1 + \sigma_2 + \sigma_3 = 2^{57.8} + 2^{156} + 2^{232.9} \approx 2^{232.9} \tag{6}$$

Where, σ_i is the maximum number of SUCs as Type-i cipher.

6 Complexity and Security Evaluation

In this section, first the security level of the SUC is bounded. After that, we discuss the expected hardware complexity of the SUC implementation.

6.1 Security Evaluation

According to Kerckhoffs's principle, attacker knows the structure of the used cipher. In SUC case, the attack's complexity is increased as the ciphers is not known. However, the general structure may be found if the GENIE is published. Otherwise, if the GENIE is not published (this allowed in the proposed concept) the attack complexity would be increased. Therefore, a successful attack on SUC consist of two phases. Firstly, seeking the structure of the SUC under attack (selected scheme Type and S-Boxes), then running a crypto attack to find the cipher parameters and finally recover the secret key of the SUC.

Theoretically, an attacker can first guess/predict the cipher-choice of the SUC with a probability of $2^{-232.9}$. The attack complexity may be reduced by applying side channel analysis to reverse engineering the particular SUC. However, as SUC is a combined HW-SW module makes reverse-engineering of both SW and HW practically more inefficient, very difficult and economically useless for low-cost mass products or systems [9].

To evaluate the security level of the resulting SUC schemes, the minimum number of "active S-Boxes", differential probability (DP), and linear approximation characteristic probability (LP) indicate and measure the resistance of the cipher structures (Type-1, Type-2, and Type-3) which use the same structure for the ciphers and their inner functions F.

In [11], the 18 round (Khudra) cipher, which uses a Type-2 structure, has at least DP/LP of 2^{-216}. By using the same security evaluation method, we can similarly come up with the results shown in Table 3.

Table 3. The resistance of different proposal of SUCs against LC and DC.

Structure	Min #active S-Box of inner function/round	DP/LP of inner function	DP/LP of cipher	Probability of successful attack
Type-1	3/8	$2^{-2\times3} = 2^{-6}$	$2^{-72} if\ r = 32$	$2^{-72} \times \sigma_1^{-1} = 2^{-129.9}$
Type-2	6/6	$2^{-2\times6} = 2^{-12}$	$2^{-216} if\ r = 18$ [11]	$2^{-216} \times \sigma_2^{-1} = 2^{-372}$
Type-3	5/4	$2^{-2\times5} = 2^{-10}$	$2^{-160} if\ r = 16$	$2^{-160} \times \sigma_3^{-1} = 2^{-392.9}$

6.2 Hardware Complexity Evaluation

For lightweight implementation, the desired SUC requires few LUTs and few DFFs in the targeted FPGA platform. Therefore, a good implementation strategy proposes the same ratio $R_{LUT/DFF}$ of LUTs and DFFs number i.e. $R_{LUT/DFF}$ is close to 1. This is resulting from the fact that most FPGAs architectures provide an easy to connect DFF with each LUT.

In what follows, we present an approximation of the hardware complexity of the SUCs resulting from the proposed GENIE design strategy. The following complexity figures can be considered:

- Each 4-bit S-Box requires 4 4-LUTs (4 inputs LUT).
- An XOR-operation between two inputs bits requires 1 4-LUT.
- A n-bit multiplexer is required for iterative ciphers. A n-bit multiplexer requires n 4-LUTs.
- n DFFs are required to store the round state and 16 DFFs are required to store the round of the inner function F.

By using the previous hardware complexity figures, the hardware resources required for a single SUC based on Type-1 design results with: 200 LUTs and 100 DFFs. For SUC based on Type-2, it requires 8 4-LUTs more in the inner function compared to Type-1. The inner function of SUC based on Type-3 requires 16 4-LUTs compared to Type-1.

An ongoing investigation is figuring out the exact required hardware resources to implement the proposed SUC designs in Microsemi SmartFusion®2 SoC FPGAs.

7   Conclusion

Creating Secret Unknown Ciphers (SUCs) includes two most challenging tasks. The first challenging task is in finding a GENIE as a smart cipher designer having low memory and execution time complexity which creates ciphers with the required security level. The second challenge, is that the created SUCs should be as small as possible in software and hardware. SUC should be accommodated possibly individually-different and randomly in small program memory and small chip logical area in the target SoC unit.

The proposed SoC FPGA-technology to realize SUCs as block ciphers in this work is an attempt to face the above two challenges as optimum as possible. The proposed mechanisms are inspired from the available technology resources expected to be available in the near future VLSI technology. The proposed GENIE as cipher creator/generator converts the device irreversibly into a physically clone- resistant entity. This happens when an unknown cipher is irreversibly created within a unit making it physically non-replaceable. The resulting light-weight ciphers are scalable in their complexity, therefore suitable for many practical future mass products applications. The designed cipher class size is cryptographically competing to cover up-to-date security level requirement for mass products in vehicular and consumer units. It is shown that the security level is scalable and can even approach and cover the post quantum security requirements.

The fact that the SUCs are not known to anybody and deal with a large class of possible ciphers, makes the number of possibilities and strategies virtually unlimited. A future work is in progress, aiming to find practical and pragmatic realizable scalable SUCs. Minimizing complexity and even costs approaching zero-hardware-complexity in existing mass products. A broad spectrum of applications of SUC-technique is expected in future consumer and vehicular environment.

Acknowledgment. The authors would like to thank Volkswagen AG as well as the German Academic Exchange Service DAAD scholarship program, the Federal Foreign Office funding by DAAD combined scholarship and support programme (STIBET) for supporting this basic research activity.

References

1. Xu, T., Potkonjak, M.: The digital bidirectional function as a hardware security primitive: architecture and applications. In: 2015 IEEE/ACM International Symposium on Low Power Electronics and Design (ISLPED), pp. 335–340. IEEE, July 2015
2. Delvaux, J., Gu, D., Peeters, R., Verbauwhede, I.: A survey on lightweight entity authentication with strong PUFs. Cryptology ePrint Archive: Report 2014/977

3. Rührmair, U., Sehnke, F., Sölter, J., Dror, G., Devadas, S., Schmidhuber, J.: Modeling attacks on physical unclonable functions. In: Proceedings of the 17th ACM Conference on Computer and Communications Security, pp. 237–249. ACM, October 2010

4. Adi, W.: Clone-resistant DNA-like secured dynamic identity. In: ECSIS Symposium on Bioinspired Learning and Intelligent Systems for Security, BLISS 2008, pp. 148–153. IEEE (2008)

5. Xu, T., Potkonjak, M.: Robust and flexible FPGA-based digital PUF. In: 2014 24th International Conference on Field Programmable Logic and Applications (FPL), pp. 1–6. IEEE, September 2014

6. Leander, G., Poschmann, A.: On the classification of 4 bit S-Boxes. In: Carlet, C., Sunar, B. (eds.) WAIFI 2007. LNCS, vol. 4547, pp. 159–176. Springer, Heidelberg (2007). https://doi. org/10.1007/978-3-540-73074-3_13

7. Saarinen, M.-J.O.: Cryptographic analysis of all 4 × 4-bit S-Boxes. In: Miri, A., Vaudenay, S. (eds.) SAC 2011. LNCS, vol. 7118, pp. 118–133. Springer, Heidelberg (2012). https://doi. org/10.1007/978-3-642-28496-0_7

8. Daemen, J., Rijmen, V.: The Design of Rijndael: AES - The Advanced Encryption Standard. Springer, Heidelberg (2001). https://doi.org/10.1007/978-3-662-04722-4

9. Fyrbiak, M., Kison, C., Jeske, M., Adi, W.: Combined HW-SW adaptive clone-resistant functions as physical security anchors. In: NASA/ESA Conference on Adaptive Hardware and Systems, AHS 2013 (2013)

10. Hoang, V.T., Rogaway, P.: On generalized feistel networks. In: Rabin, T. (ed.) CRYPTO 2010. LNCS, vol. 6223, pp. 613–630. Springer, Heidelberg (2010). https://doi.org/10.1007/ 978-3-642-14623-7_33

11. Kolay, S., Mukhopadhyay, D.: Khudra: a new lightweight block cipher for FPGAs. In: Chakraborty, R.S., Matyas, V., Schaumont, P. (eds.) SPACE 2014. LNCS, vol. 8804, pp. 126–145. Springer, Cham (2014). https://doi.org/10.1007/978-3-319-12060-7_9

12. Wu, J., O'Neill, M.: On foundation and construction of physical unclonable functions. IACR Cryptology ePrint Archive 2010, p. 171 (2010)

13. Mars, A., et al.: Random stream cipher as a PUF-like identity in FPGA environment. In: Proceedings of 2017 7th International Conference on Emerging Security Technologies, EST 2017 (2017)

14. Adi, W., et al.: Generic identification protocols by deploying Secret Unknown Ciphers (SUCs). In: 2017 IEEE International Conference on Consumer Electronics - Taiwan, ICCE-TW 2017, pp. 255–256 (2017)

A Secure and Efficient File System Access Control Mechanism (FlexFS)

Jihane Najar$^{(\boxtimes)}$ and Vassilis Prevelakis

Institute of Computer and Network Engineering, TU Braunschweig,
Braunschweig, Germany
{jihanen,prevelakis}@ida.ing.tu-bs.de

Abstract. The FlexFS approach provides an effective credential-based access control mechanism while ensuring file access performance equivalent to that of the normal file system. This is achieved by decoupling the file system naming and access control layer from the block I/O layer. By intercepting and redefining file system API calls in libc (e.g. open(2)), we allow any existing executable to use FlexFS while keeping FlexFS as a user-level system without any changes to the kernel. This allows for rapid experimentation without impacting system stability.

Keywords: Access control · File system · Credentials · Opencall · Wrapper functions

1 Introduction

File systems traditionally serve two high-level purposes: naming and access control. These are in addition to the low-level mechanism that deal with the actual storage of the file contents and have to deal with fast access, storage optimization, recovery etc. At the high-level, file systems enable users to organize their data in separate files by allowing these files to be named and organized. The file system provides a convenient representation of the data layout which is maintained by the operating system. There are wide varieties of file system implementations that describe different ways to organize the data and different ways to look at the data. These include the traditional hierarchical point of view, the database point of view and so on. The hierarchical organization is the most common file system organization and is found in systems such as DOS, Windows, Linux and so on.

Moreover, file systems typically include extensive access control mechanisms that ensure that only suitably authorized users are granted access to a given file. However, in many file systems, the access control mechanism is deeply integrated in the file system code making changes to it difficult and intrusive. Worse, they usually require changes to the programming API and modifications to the kernel itself. For example in Unix/Linux systems, to open a file, one has to access it, i.e. find a path through the directory structure of the file system that allows the

© Springer Nature Switzerland AG 2019
A. P. Fournaris et al. (Eds.): IOSec 2018, LNCS 11398, pp. 15–26, 2019.
https://doi.org/10.1007/978-3-030-12085-6_2

user to open the file. At this stage, access control is handled by the i-node itself. Since there is no user-accessible mechanism to open a file given its i-node, both mechanisms must allow access for a file to be opened. Eventually, the original Unix access control mechanisms for the file system were deemed to be inadequate and additional permission bits (e.g. the immutable bit) were introduced as well as access control lists (ACL).

The problem with this approach, however, is that it increases the size of the kernel while providing multiple ways for a file to be accessed thus confusing the programmer and thus creating loopholes that may be exploited to bypass the intent of the security of the system. For example, temporary access to a file may allow a malicious user to create a hard link to that file. Then the path-based access control mechanism will be ineffective limiting the protection to the access control offered by the i-node and ACL. In addition, numerous race conditions are described in the literature [5].

Our approach is different though the use of trust management credentials. It has to distinct facets, the first introduces a new access control paradigm based on Trust Management, while the second allows the access control layer to compliment the existing file system code, thus enjoying all the low-level facilities of the underlying file system (access, speed, storage etc). The access control layer directly authorizes actions, rather than divide the authorization task into authentication and access control. Unlike traditional credentials, which bind keys to principals, trust management credentials bind keys to the authorization to perform certain tasks. FlexFS, uses trust management credentials to identify: (1) files being stored; (2) users (not in the unix sence, but as keys that authorize actions); and (3) conditions under which their file access is allowed. Users share files by delegating access rights, issuing credentials in the style of traditional capabilities.

An earlier version of this mechanism was used in our Distributed Credential FileSystem (DisCFS) [12]. In addition our mechanism may be used to provide alternate file system organizations by moving the naming and access control component of the file system to a user-level process. The advantage of this approach is that multiple access control mechanisms may co-exist in a given system, each customized to the security requirements of a particular application. However, we can ensure that access from a specific application to a class of files may be performed only via the specific access control mechanism. Thus an attacker may not "pick and chose" the access control mechanism that will grant her access, but is forced to negotiate access via the specified mechanism. Finally, FlexFS improves on the earlier work by limiting the security overhead to the open(2) call thus allowing the fast native file I/O mechanism in the kernel to be used.

The rest of the paper is organized as follows. A description of related work is presented in the next section. In Sect. 3, we present the architecture of the FlexFS access control mechanism. In Sect. 4, we describe the implementation details. In Sect. 5, we present measurements of the prototype. Finally in Sect. 6 we provide our analysis of FlexFS, and future work.

2 Related Work

2.1 Access Control

Access Control is the process or mechanism by which users are granted access and certain privileges to specific resources, applications and system. Access control defines a set of conditions or criteria to control how users interact with the system and its resources. There are three main access Control models [22]: Mandatory access control model, Discretionary access control model and Role based access control models.

Another way of simplifying the management of access rights is to store the access control matrix, a column at a time, along with the resource to which the column refers. This is called an access control list or ACL.

An ACL is attached with every object in the system. It lists all the access control entries which are authorized to access the resource along with their access rights. Different authentication mechanisms, such as Kerberos [9] or X.509 certificate, allow ACLs to be used in a network environment. An ACL is an unforgeable token that identifies a resource and lists the access rights granted to the holder of the ACL. Anyone holding a copy of the ACL can access to a particular system object with the access rights specified by the ACL.

ACLs are also useful in case where a particular user is not a member of group, but the creator of the group wants to give him some read or write access without making this user a member of the group.

2.2 Existing Files Systems

File management is essential in any file system which uses the access control service to enforce file access permissions. This way, it's the ability of a system to grant or reject access to a protected resource. This design has seen many implementations. Perhaps the quintessential implementation of this design is the Berkeley Software Distribution Fast File System (BSD FFS, or just FFS). It is a file system supported by many Unix and Unix-like operating systems.

Although network file systems such as NFS [18] and AFS [8] are the most popular mechanisms for sharing files in tightly-administered domains, crossing administrative boundaries creates numerous problems (e.g., merging distinct Kerberos realms or NIS domains). The developers of the Athena [17], Hesiod [6] and Bones [19] systems recognize and address some of these problems.

SFS [11] introduces the notion of self-certifying pathnames, which consists of the file server's location, e.g., a host name or an IP address and a HostID that tells the client how to certify a secure channel to the server. In this way, SFS needs no separate key management machinery to communicate securely with file servers.

Encrypting file systems such as CFS [2] uses DES for data encryption. To protect a directory, a cryptographic key is associated by the user. Thus, all the files which are included in this directory (as well as their pathname component) are encrypted and decrypted without further user intervention.

Capability File Names [13] is an access control mechanism that uses self-certifying file names as sparse capabilities to control access to files. With CapaFS there is no need for a system administrator intervention. To share a file, users need only to communicate the file name. However, once a capability is communicated, there is no way to control access to the file in the future without employing additional mechanisms. While the user can always copy the file to avoid access control issues in the future, she will not receive any updates to the content of the file.

WebFS is part of the larger WebOS [23] project at UC Berkeley. It is a global filesystem that uses user-level HTTP servers to transfer data, along with a kernel module that implements the file system. It uses X.509 certificates to identify users and transfer privileges. Each file is associated with an ACL that enumerates which users have read, write, or execute permission on individual files.

DisCFS [12] is the most closely system related to our work. It uses credentials to identify both the files stored in the file system and the users that are permitted to access them, as well as the circumstances under which such access is allowed. Furthermore, users can delegate access rights simply by issuing new credentials, providing a natural and very scalable way of sharing information.

Some other file systems like XFS [20], ZFS [16], and BtrFS [15] concentrate on the block layer: XFS is a filesystem designed to achieve high scalability in term of IO thread, number of disk and file size. It uses B-tree of extents to manage disk space. ZFS is designed to be a file system that scales from a few networked computers to several thousand machines. ZFS retrieves the data block from the remote machine instead of going to the disk for a block of data already in one of the machine memories. And BTRFS combined ideas with COW friendly B-trees [14] to create a new Linux filesystem.

The problem with the existing systems is that all the access control mechanism are enabled at the same time. This is not the case for our system which offers multiple ways to carry out access control and multiple ways to organize files. In our system we can choose the most appropriate naming scheme or access control scheme and the application will have to use only this mechanism, while retaining the ability to use the block layer mechanism of the underlying file system.

3 Architecture

3.1 Traditional Unix File System

The UNIX file system is a descending hierarchy of files. All the files and directories are under the root. So to access to a file we need to be able to reach it via the path (i.e. at least execute permission for all directories), and we need to have some appropriate access permissions for the file (e.g. read for read only etc.).

In a traditional Unix File System, access to a file is governed not only by the file's permissions, but by the hierarchy of permissions of all of the directories above it. Access control in these systems consists of both permissions (read, write, execute) and ownership (user, group) information, located in the metadata for each file. This was not sufficient, more flexible permission scheme called an Access Control List or (ACLs) was added. In this scheme, specific permissions may be granted to specific accounts, rather than just to groups. It provides better file security by defining file permissions for the file owner, file group, other, specific users and groups, and default permissions for each of those categories. ACLs (access control lists) can be used as an extension of the traditional permission concept for file system objects. With ACLs, permissions can be defined more flexibly than the traditional permission concept allows. For example, if we wanted everyone in a group to be able to read a file, we would simply give group read permissions on that file. Now, assume we wanted only one person in the group to be able to write to that file. That level of file security is not providing by the standard UNIX. However, this dilemma is perfect for ACLs. But because with ACLs we are dealing with usernames, no one other than the owner can change the Access Control List and delegates others access to a file.

3.2 FlexFS

The FlexFs uses credentials to identify both the files stored in the file system and the users that are permitted to access them, as well as the circumstances under which such access is allowed. To open a file, we need to request it and to have the appropriate access control policies. The request should be signed with the client's private key and must be associated by other credentials that form a row of trust which link the client's key to a key that is trusted by the system.

The system gets a request and a bunch of credentials. Each credential transfer trust from one key to another. The conditions for the transfer of trust are expressed in the policy inside the credential. The request is signed with the key of the requester and the credentials have to provide a chain from the requester key and a key that the system trusts with respect to the file.

It is a policy based mechanism for authentication and access control of files. Policy is made to have a rich File Access Control mechanism and it will be possible to change it. It means that making changes to the Access Control mechanism doesn't imply change the kernel, but modify the user-level process. Because FlexFS is very flexible, it's possible to add more than one server.

It is a filesystem with files and directories. They contain an access control credential. The content of the file is stored elsewhere contrarily to the traditional Unix FS access control which prevents direct access to file content. In FlexFS, the open systemcall contacts a user-level policy manager (UPM). The User-Level Policy Manager is a separate process which handles authentication and access control. One or more UPM can exist in the system. The UPM decides which file to open and whether to grant request. It opens then the file, passes the file descriptor from one process to another. All the efficiencies of Unix-based I/O are preserved. It's not developing a new file system machinery, it's just a way to provide access control to files.

To express access rights and the diverse conditions under which these are granted, we need to formulate policies. There are a number of possible choices such as PolicyMaker [4], KeyNote [3], QCM [7], and SPKI [10]. In our system, we decided to use the KeyNote trust management system for this purpose.

KeyNote is based on credentials and policies. It defines a specific language for credentials, which is designed for policy and request evaluation. Credentials are signed assertions, while unsigned assertions present policies. Both of them are managed by the KeyNote Compliance Checker: that is the process of deciding whether a proposed action conforms to policy. Compliance Checker represents the basic service provided by KeyNote.

4   Implementation

Our prototype implementation of FlexFS allows users to create the delegation credentials.

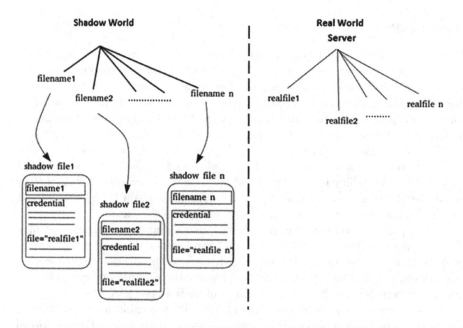

Fig. 1. Difference between shadow world and real world

The server is relied on a user-level policy manager (UPM) to handle authentication and access control. It creates the delegation credential in a shadow file as seen in Fig. 1 and sends it to the client. The communication between the server and users is done over a Unix sockets. When the client wants to access to the file, he must have enough credential like the one shown in Fig. 2. This credential is issued by the server to a specific user as identified by the public key appearing in the Authorizer field for the server and the public key appearing in the Licensees field for the client. The client must send his request signed with his private key accompanied with the credential given by the server which contains all information to determine what permissions should be granted.

```
keynote-version: 2
authorizer: "<Server's Public key>"
licensees: "<Client's public key>"
conditions: app_domain == "file descriptor" && fname == "filename"&&
            access == "r" -> "true";
signature:  "<Signed by the Server>"
```

Fig. 2. An example of KeyNote credential

A wrapper version of the open is called in this case. It sits between applications and libc as shown in Fig. 3. Inside the wrapper, the credential is read, the request is formulated and signed, and then both of them are sent to the server. However, the request must be accompanied by the challenge given by the server. The goal is to provide upwards compatibility with existing programs without changing the source or even recompiling.

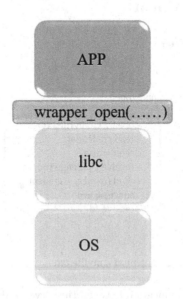

Fig. 3. The wrapper version of open(2)

After receiving the credential and the request, the server extracts the necessary information of the requested file. It uses KeyNote to validate it. If it conforms to policy, it opens the file, sends the file descriptor back and then closes the file. In this case, the client doesn't open the file itself, it opens a shadow file with information that allow the actual file server to be consulted, the real file is opened by the file server and then the file descriptor is sent back. The process is described in Fig. 4.

In our prototype, we used a shell environment in Linux called LD_PRELOAD [21]. It allows our shared library, that overrides open(2) functions, to be loaded before any other library including glibc.

FlexFS is implemented by converting a name to a file descriptor. This is achieved by creating a layer between the file system and the user. It provides the user a way to access files using the new mapping (the mapping between names and file descriptor). The file identified by a name by the user, will be identified with a shadow file and while the actual file will be opened by the server. When a file is requested and permissions are granted, the client will receive the file descriptor back.

To send an open file descriptor from one process to another, libancillary [1] is used. It provides an easy interface to pass file descriptors between processes. This library can send and receive one or more file descriptors via a Unix socket. In our case, the client has not enough rights to open a file directly, so another process which is the file server will open it and send its file descriptor back to the client.

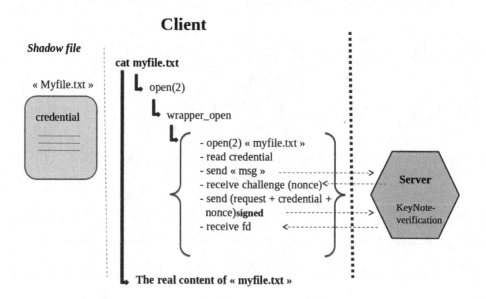

Fig. 4. Communication between the server and the client

An important characteristic of returning a file descriptor to an open file is that it will not need the server anymore. Even if the file is deleted, it will remain in existence for the client until the last file descriptor referring to it is closed. This means that the server can not take back or deny the access.

Nevertheless, by passing the file descriptor to the client, the FlexFS server is no longer in the loop and does not impose any additional overheads while the file is being used.

5   Evaluation

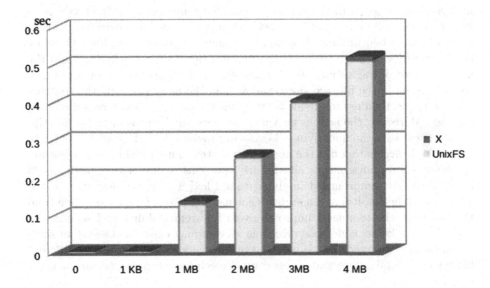

Fig. 5. Performance comparison between FlexFS and UnixFS

We evaluated our implementation by measuring the time spent to sort a file and compared it with the standard Unix File System. We used Linux command "time" for the measurement. The time command gives statistics about how long the sort command takes to run. The above measurement was deployed in a DELL Laptop Intel® Core™ i7-7820HQ CPU @ 2.90 GHz, with 8 GB of memory (RAM), running on Linux (Ubuntu 16.04 LTS). We have repeated the test 20 times. Figure 5 presents the average elapsed time.

As shown in Fig. 5, our system imposes overhead that is roughly that same regardless of the size of the file or the use of the file once it has been opened. Most of the overhead comes from policy evaluation, credential evaluation and signature verification of the credentials. Once the file is opened then the normal Unix I/O overhead is increment, which is the same as with the standard mechanism. Furthermore, to reduce the cost of policy evaluation, various optimization techniques, such as caching verified credentials and policy, may be used.

6   Analysis - Discussion

It is important to note that the proposed mechanism is intended to allow experimentation and debugging of the access control mechanism. If the file is accessible to the user-id of a malicious user, then she can bypass the standard library and access the system call directly, thus obtaining access to the file. To protect against such an attack, the files are owned by the server process and their permissions are such that other users cannot open these files. In addition, the directory under which these files are stored is accessible only by the server process so that access via the traditional file access mechanisms is blocked.

A key characteristic of FlexFS is that once the file is opened, a standard Unix file descriptor is given to the process. From that moment onwards FlexFS is no longer involved. As a result, file access is then performed via native mechanisms and file system benchmarks show no performance degradation in file I/O. Especially with files that are used extensively after opening (e.g. when sorting) the increased cost of the initial open(2) represents a small percentage of the overall cost of accessing the file. On the negative side, the user may copy the contents of the file, and then use it outside FlexFS, thus bypassing FlexFS on subsequent accesses. Moreover, the actions that may be performed on the open file descriptor are those that the underlying file system provides. E.g. if we wish to enforce append-only access to a file, the normal file system must provide such a feature.

Server compromise means all files are lost. This is similar to what happens if the kernel is compromised implying that FlexFS server is now part of the TCB. Nevertheless, it may be argued that moving a lot of file access code from the kernel to the user level improves overall system stability and security by shrinking the kernel code base. Multiple servers may exist on the system since the name of the server may be included in the shadow file. This allows different file system organizations and access control mechanisms to co-exist in the same system.

The stub mechanism is used as the means to achieve binary compatibility with existing programs and system utilities. It also allows one-to-one comparisons with other mechanisms. It is therefore a convenience and is not part of the security of the system. If a program decides to bypass the FlexFS library stubs and access glibc, or even the kernel system calls, directly, it will still have to provide the necessary credentials to the FlexFS server to access the file since the owner of the file is the FlexFS sever and not the user.

Our future plans include experimentation with alternative organizations and access control mechanisms customized to each specific application.

7   Conclusion

In this paper we presented a new access control mechanism; credential-based mechanism. The FlexFS prototype separates policy from the access control mechanism and allows the credentials to be implemented at the library call level. In our framework users can make some changes on a file if they have the necessary credentials. In this case access to the file will be reached by the file descriptor from the server.

We have shown that this mechanism can be used to augment the traditional Unix-style look-and-feel, including ACLs. These may be implemented by delegation credentials that define who and under which circumstances may access a file. We may even include conditions such as time-of-day (file not accessible outside office hours), working days versus weekends or holidays, system status (e.g. loaded/unloaded), DEFCON and so on.

This mechanism may be used to provide an alternate file system organization by moving the naming and access control component of the file system to a user-level process.

The system performance was evaluated and the overhead comes from policy evaluation, credential evaluation and signature verification.

Acknowledgement. This work was supported by the European Commission Horizon 2020 through project H2020-DS-SC7-2017 "THREAT-ARREST" under Grant Agreement No. 786890.

References

1. Ancillary library. https://www.normalesup.org/~george/comp/libancillary/. Accessed 18 July 2018
2. Blaze, M.: A cryptographic file system for UNIX. In: Proceedings of the 1st ACM Conference on Computer and Communications Security, pp. 9–16. ACM (1993)
3. Blaze, M., Feigenbaum, J., Ioannidis, J., Keromytis, A.: The KeyNote trust-management system version 2. Technical report (1999)
4. Blaze, M., Feigenbaum, J., Lacy, J.: Decentralized trust management. In: Proceedings of the 1996 IEEE Symposium on Security and Privacy, pp. 164–173. IEEE (1996)
5. Corp, M.: CWE-367: Time-of-check time-of-use (TOCTOU) race condition. https://cwe.mitre.org/data/definitions/367.html. Accessed 29 Mar 2018
6. Dyer, S.P.: The Hesiod name server. In: USENIX Winter, pp. 183–189 (1988)
7. Gunter, C.A., Jim, T.: Policy-directed certificate retrieval. Softw.: Pract. Exp. **30**(15), 1609–1640 (2000)
8. Nichols, D.A., et al.: Scale and performance in a distributed file system. ACM Trans. Comput. Syst. (TOCS) **6**(1), 51–81 (1988)
9. Kohl, J., Neuman, C.: The Kerberos network authentication service (V5). Technical report (1993)
10. Lampson, B., Rivest, R., Thomas, B., Ylonen, T.: SPKI certificate theory (1999)
11. Mazieres, D., Kaminsky, M., Kaashoek, M.F., Witchel, E.: Separating key management from file system security. ACM SIGOPS Oper. Syst. Rev. **33**, 124–139 (1999)
12. Miltchev, S., Prevelakis, V., Ioannidis, S., Ioannidis, J., Keromytis, A.D., Smith, J.M.: Secure and flexible global file sharing. In: USENIX Annual Technical Conference, FREENIX Track, pp. 165–178 (2003)
13. Regan, J.T., Jensen, C.D.: Capability file names: separating authorisation from user management in an internet file system. In: USENIX Security Symposium (2001)

14. Rodeh, O.: B-trees, shadowing, and clones. ACM Trans. Storage (TOS) **3**(4), 2 (2008)
15. Rodeh, O., Bacik, J., Mason, C.: BTRFS: the Linux B-tree filesystem. ACM Trans. Storage (TOS) **9**(3), 9 (2013)
16. Rodeh, O., Teperman, A.: zFS-a scalable distributed file system using object disks. In: Proceedings of the 20th IEEE/11th NASA Goddard Conference on Mass Storage Systems and Technologies, MSST 2003, pp. 207–218. IEEE (2003)
17. Rosenstein, M.A., Geer Jr., D.E., Levine, P.J.: The Athena service management system. In: USENIX Winter, pp. 203–211 (1988)
18. Sandberg, R., Goldberg, D., Kleiman, S., Walsh, D., Lyon, B.: Design and implementation of the sun network filesystem. In: Proceedings of the Summer USENIX Conference, pp. 119–130 (1985)
19. Schönwälder, J., Langendörfer, H.: Administration of large distributed UNIX LANs with BONES. In: Proceedings of the World Conference On Tools and Techniques for System Administration, Networking, and Security. Citeseer (1993)
20. Sweeney, A., Doucette, D., Hu, W., Anderson, C., Nishimoto, M., Peck, G.: Scalability in the XFS file system. In: USENIX Annual Technical Conference, vol. 15 (1996)
21. Tsantekidis, M., Prevelakis, V.: Library-level policy enforcement
22. Ubale Swapnaja, A., Modani Dattatray, G., Apte Sulabha, S.: Analysis of DAC MAC RBAC access control based models for security. Analysis **104**(5) (2014)
23. Vahdat, M.A., Anderson, T.E., Kubiatowicz, J.D.: Operating System Services for Wide-Area Applications. Citeseer, Princeton (1998)

Protecting Cloud-Based CIs: Covert Channel Vulnerabilities at the Resource Level

Tsvetoslava Vateva-Gurova[1]([⊠]), Salman Manzoor[1], Ruben Trapero[2], and Neeraj Suri[1]

[1] CS Department, Technische Universität Darmstadt, Darmstadt, Germany
{vateva,salman,suri}@deeds.informatik.tu-darmstadt.de
[2] Atos Research and Innovation, Madrid, Spain
ruben.trapero@atos.net

Abstract. Critical Infrastructures (CIs) increasingly leverage Cloud computing given its benefits of on-demand scalability, high availability and cost efficiency. However, the Cloud is typically characterized by the co-location of users from varied security domains that also use shared computing resources. This introduces a number of resource/architecture-level vulnerabilities. For example, the usage of a basic shared storage component, such as a memory cache, can expose the entire Cloud system to security risks such as covert-channel attacks. The success of these exploits depends on various execution environment properties. Thus, providing means to assess the feasibility of these attacks in a specific execution environment and enabling postmortem analysis is needed.

While attacks at the architectural level represent a potent vulnerability to exfiltrate information, the low-level often get neglected with techniques such as intrusion detection focused more on the high-level network/middleware threats. Interestingly, cache-based covert-channel attacks are typically not detectable by traditional intrusion detection systems as covert channels do not obey any access rights or other security policies. This paper focuses on the information provided at the low architectural level to cope with the cache-based covert-channel threat. We propose the usage of feasibility metrics collected at the low level to monitor the core-private cache covert channel and, infer information regarding the probability of a covert-channel exploit happening. We also illustrate the applicability of the proposed feasibility metrics in a use case.

Keywords: Information leakage · Scheduling · Side channels · Covert channels · Feasibility

1 Introduction

For its cost efficiency, high availability and on-demand scaling, Cloud computing has become prevalent for myriad applications. According to Gartner, Inc. by

© Springer Nature Switzerland AG 2019
A. P. Fournaris et al. (Eds.): IOSec 2018, LNCS 11398, pp. 27–38, 2019.
https://doi.org/10.1007/978-3-030-12085-6_3

2020 [2], a "no-cloud" policy will be rare in the corporate world. Moreover, a survey conducted in 2014 by Healthcare Information and Management Systems Society (HIMMS) Analytics [4] confirms the increasingly wide-spread adoption of Cloud services in critical sectors such as Healthcare. As Critical Infrastructures (CIs) increasingly leverage the Cloud computing for its scalability, large-scale connectivity and high availability, consequently, the security vulnerabilities of the Cloud affect the security of CIs driving the need for sophisticated preventive measures.

Covert- and side-channel attacks (CCAs and SCAs) have long been considered a system security threat, and their prevalence is increasing given the shared resources model employed by the Cloud[1], as demonstrated in [11,16,23]. The lack of approaches to address SCAs and CCAs practically without introducing significant performance overhead or, the need of additional hardware which increases the financial cost worsen the situation. SCAs and CCAs can pose a threat to any system performing, e.g., sensitive cryptographic operations, including critical infrastructure hardware that provides shared access to users of different security domains. As the Cloud computing becomes prevalent, the risk of covert-channel attacks or side-channel attacks stemming from the usage of shared hardware should not be underestimated.

Varied resources exhibiting observable side effects can be used as a covert or side channel[2]. SCAs and CCAs can be conducted by analyzing the physical effects of the hardware being used, e.g., power analysis (cf., [5,15]), acoustic noise (cf., [3]) or electromagnetic emanations (cf. [1]), or through spying software. While the attacks based on the analysis of the physical effects of a device might require additional measuring equipment or proximity to the device being attacked, the software-based approaches are more practical. They can be conducted, e.g., by periodically timing the accesses to a resource that is being used by both an attacker and a victim, and do not require special privileges for the attacker. Whereas an SCA is characterized by an attacker spying on the victim's usage of the shared resource, a CCA is characterized by two cooperating attackers using the shared resource to transmit information. In the latter case, one of the attackers accesses the shared resource in a specific predefined way to transfer the data to the other attacker.

With our focus on core-private caches as a covert channel (CC), it has already been demonstrated that the properties of the execution environment affect the feasibility of SCAs and CCAs [19,26]. Among these properties is the CPU scheduling that might allow for a fine-granular observation of the victim's cache usage [7,18,20,26]. There is a strong correlation between the scheduling of the attacker directly after the victim in a side-channel attack, and the success of the core-private side-channel attacks employing the Prime+Probe strategy. Thus, available scheduling traces can be used to provide valuable information regard-

---

[1] CCAs and SCAs represent a threat to the Cloud settings despite the presumed secure isolation among the Cloud users.

[2] The terms covert channel and side channel are used interchangeably within the paper.

ing the feasibility of a core-private cache-based CCA or SCA for a given system, as analyzing the effect of the scheduling algorithms on these attacks directly seems to be infeasible due to the involved indeterminism. In addition, abusing the scheduler is often a prerequisite for a successful covert-channel exploit, as the attacker needs frequent observations on the activities of the victim or the cooperating attacker. This is usually achieved through Inter-processor Interrupts (IPIs). For instance, the authors of [26] use IPIs to collect fine-granular data on the victim's cache usage. Such information can be applied to assess the feasibility of SCAs and CCAs in a particular system and conduct post-mortem analysis without ignoring the load on the system and the properties of the execution environment.

Contributions and Paper Organization

This paper addresses the effects the scheduling has on the covert-channel exploitation using the Prime+Probe strategy [10,16,26]. While contemporary research often focuses on Flush+Reload-based SCAs and CCAs [8,24], this coverage is limited, as this class of attacks depends on the usage of features such as memory deduplication which are disabled in the most Cloud settings [21,22]. The CPU scheduling enabling proper synchronization upon the usage of the covert channel is a cornerstone for the success of the conducted attack. As the core-private cache can be seen as a memory-less communication channel, each process intervening with the cache erases the cache footprint and with that the data conveyed by the footprint. In this case the attacker and the victim are not synchronized which affects the quality of the obtained data.

Having this in mind, we propose the monitoring of three scheduling-related metrics to infer the feasibility of a cache-based exploit. The frequency of inter-processor interrupts and busy waiting and the number of successive scheduling of two processes on the same CPU core are valuable sources of information regarding the probability of an attack happening. To this end, we propose to use the scheduling traces for post-mortem analysis or feasibility assessment of a covert-channel exploit. We conduct our analysis based on a case study by considering the feasibility of a L1 covert-channel attack based on the Prime+Probe strategy.

Paper Contributions: Overall, our contributions are threefold:

1. We conduct a systematic abstract information-level characterization of scheduling considerations for side- and covert-channel attacks,
2. We propose architectural level metrics, based on IPIs, busy waiting and successive scheduling to assess the feasibility of a cache exploit (in Sect. 4),
3. We demonstrate of the applicability of the proposed metrics to monitor the CC in a case study (in Sect. 5).

Key Findings: The experimental results demonstrate the utility of the chosen metrics as indicators for possible successful transmission over the cache as a covert channel. This ascertains the usefulness of the usage of the low-level information to extract feasibility metrics for cache-based covert-channel exploits.

2   Related Work

This section reviews the related work in the area of side- and covert-channel attack approaches, and discusses the state-of-the-art research related to the scheduling effect on these attacks.

Among the most popular strategies for conducting SCAs and CCAs are Prime+Probe (employed in, e.g., [10,16,26]) and Flush+Reload (demonstrated in, e.g., [8,24]). They have been applied to leak information at different cache levels. Prime+Probe had been leveraged only to target exploiting the core-private caches [23,26] due to the previously unknown or undocumented Last Level Cache (LLC) addressing scheme of modern processors in the past. However, the reverse engineering of the LLC complex addressing scheme, described in [13,25], made even the Prime+Probe attacks targetting the LLC practical [10].

The Flush+Reload attacks represent a powerful mean for exfiltrating secret data. However, their practical applicability is limited due to the assumptions behind this class of attacks. Flush+Reload attacks rely on the usage of features such as memory deduplication that enables the usage of the same memory pages by two processes that might be adversaries. As these attacks can be easily prevented by disabling the memory deduplication feature, they are not in the focus of our work. Actually, this measure has already been applied by many Cloud providers, as noted in [21,22].

The effect of the synchronization between the attackers in a CCA and the attacker and the victim in an SCA has already been studied. Hu [6] proposed to use fuzzy time system clocks to disable the proper synchronization and reduce the capacity of a CC. However, this approach is not practical, as it poses restrictions on the execution environment of other processes, as well.

The authors of [11] also discussed the varied factors that influence the feasibility of cache-based CCAs, among them the synchronization of the covert communication. Based on that observation, the authors defined three types of errors in the CC in [11] distinguishing between substitution errors, insertion errors and deletion errors.

In [26], Zhang et al. abused the scheduler by issuing interrupts to obtain fine-granularity of their observations on the victim's actions. The synchronization (i.e., the scheduling effect) has been reported as a challenge or even feasibility aspect for conducting SCAs and CCAs in varied papers e.g., [11,19,26]. The scheduling policy is used even as a defense mechanism against cache-based SCAs in the research described in [18].

Although works related to the impact of scheduling on the accesses to the CC exist, there is no comprehensive, systematic analysis on the topic that might be applied on varied systems to analyze the covert-channel threat using the scheduling traces.

3   System and Attacker Models

We now present the system model serving as a basis for the paper. Additionally, the relevant SCA and CCA attacker models are detailed. This paper focuses on the core-private cache as a CC between two processes. Thus, our system model, depicted in Fig. 1, consists of the CPU and the core-private cache, as being part of the CPU and providing the basis for the covert communication.

A hierarchy of caches, targeting frequently used data, is used to alleviate the speed bottleneck caused by the slow accesses to the main memory. Current architectures are characterized by more than one cache levels where the Level 1 (L1) cache is the fastest and the smallest cache. It is divided into L1 data cache and L1 instruction cache and is core-private. The Level 2 (L2) cache is unified (i.e., storing data and instructions) and, might be core-private or shared depending on the architecture. The largest and slowest is the LLC. Some architectures might also have only L1 (core-private) and last level (shared) caches. As the CPU scheduling is the focus of this work, the CPU scheduler assigning the processes to the CPU cores and with that granting the access to the respective core-private cache, is a significant part of the system model.

Due to the timing differences for the data accesses, it can be inferred where the requested data has been stored (main memory or certain cache level). If the data has to be fetched from the main memory and to be copied into the cache, accessing it takes longer. This is referred to as a cache miss. On the contrary, if the data is already in the cache, accessing it is faster and is referred to as a cache hit. Namely the timing differences in case of a cache hit and cache miss can be analyzed and exploited to leak secret information though the cache as a CC. Through such an analysis, by frequently sampling the cache, an attacker can infer the cache access pattern or cache footprint of another process and can deduce information regarding other process' cache usage which can be further analyzed. In such a scenario, the attacker can be an arbitrary non-privileged process using the same core-private cache as the other process.

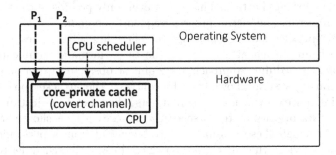

Fig. 1. System model.

This paper focuses on the usage of the CC in both SCAs and CCAs. Although these attacks use the same communication channel, there are slight differences in their attacker models. On one hand, a SCA is characterized by a victim and by an attacker spying on the victims usage of the cache to leak, e.g., secret keys, whereas in the CCA two attackers exchange information over the cache, e.g., a message. In both cases, the leaked information is in the form of cache footprints that are being collected during the attack, and analyzed after that to decode their meaning. For simplicity, from now on, the party leaving the cache footprint (e.g., the victim in an SCA) is referred to as a *sender* for both types of the attack, and the party decoding the cache footprint (the attacker in an SCA) is called the *receiver* for both attacks. Any other process that interacts with the cache causes noise in the channel from the perspective of the sender and the receiver.

4   CPU Scheduling and Feasibility Metrics

This section discusses on the effect of the scheduling on the exploitability of the cache as a covert channel using the Prime+Probe strategy.

4.1   Scheduling Considerations

The proposed metrics are related to the scheduling of the attacker process(es). Thus, in the next paragraphs we present scheduling issues relevant for the successful attack deployment, and detail what are the scheduling considerations that have to be taken into account for the metrics derivation.

Abusing the Scheduler. Zhang et al. demonstrated a L1 side-channel attack in a Cloud scenario in [26]. In their paper, the authors propose using a third party (an additional VM) to issue IPIs, so that the attacker can be scheduled frequently enough after the victim. This enables the attacker to collect fine-granular observations over the victim's cache usage. This approach plays a major role in the demonstrated attack. This is, however, only possible if the third party process can interrupt the victim process frequently enough.

From this perspective, non-preemptive scheduling approaches tend to be more secure against such attacks. Still, due to performance implications, the non-preemptive scheduling approaches are almost obsolete in user space of the modern operating systems nowadays. In contrast, the attacker process could even try to influence on which CPU core it gets scheduled, to adjust under given circumstances its priority or to be scheduled according to a chosen scheduling scheme [9]. Although these possibilities are beneficial from a performance and usability point of view, they increase the risk of abusing the scheduler to achieve better synchronization over the usage of the covert channel.

Synchronisation and Atomicity of Operations. As already discussed, the synchronization between the involved parties in a side-channel attack and a covert-channel attack, i.e., between the victim and an attacker in the SCA scenario and between the two cooperating attackers in the CCA scenario, is crucial for the success of the attacks. Ideally, the receiver is scheduled directly after the sender. Moreover, the receiver has to be scheduled after the sender has completed its operation to retain the atomicity of the operations. If the sender gets preempted in the middle of the sending, the receiver will not be able to decode the data.

The same applies if the sender uses the CPU for too long while performing more than one operations. Then, the receiver would not be able to collect all the possible observations. The times the receiver and sender should be scheduled depend on the execution times of the sending and receiving operations to achieve optimal attack results. It is also important that the receiver and sender processes are of roughly the same priority so that they have similar chances to be scheduled.

4.2   Low-Level Feasibility Metrics

Having in mind the scheduling effect on the feasibility of side-channel attack or covert-channel attack, we propose to monitor the scheduling related metrics to exfiltrate information regarding the usage of the covert channel. For this purpose, we propose using three feasibility metrics. They are briefly discussed below:

Successive Scheduling (SS). The successive scheduling of two processes can be used as an indicator for the feasibility of the usage of the core-private cache as a covert channel. As the receiver has to be scheduled directly after the sender to obtain information, this metric can be applied as a feasibility indicator. We can monitor SS for a process with suspicious behaviour.

Busy Waiting (BW). In a Prime+Probe attack, the synchronisation is usually done through busy waiting. After each measurement, the attacker process yields the CPU and during attacker's busy waiting the victim should get scheduled. This is a very important step in the attack to guarantee the atomicity of operations. Thus, BW can be used not only as a feasibility metric, but also to identify the processes with suspicious behaviour for which the SS metric should be considered.

Interprocessor Interrupts (IPIs). IPIs can be used to abuse the scheduler to grant frequent access to the cache. Thus the number of IPIs over predefined time span can be monitored as an indicator that an attack, as the one described in [26], might be happening. By considering these feasibility metrics, a system administrator can derive a threshold, and monitor for the feasibility of an attack. This is a lightweight approach to monitor ICT systems, among them also CIs, for possible cache-based covert-channel exploits, and enhance the security of these systems.

5   Covert Channel Monitoring and Application Scenario

In this section, we analyze empirically the utility of the proposed feasibility metrics, by conducting post-mortem analysis based on a covert-channel exploit.

For that, we deployed a CCA in three different scenarios using varied background load levels, and collected the proposed metrics during the attack. Additionally, for comparison purposes we gathered the feasibility metrics in a non-attacked system with varied background load levels. The experiments were done in Debian Stretch Operating System. For each experiment, we measured the success of the attack and extracted the proposed metrics using the available hardware performance counters.

5.1 Implementation Details

We implemented a Prime+Probe CCA consisting of a sender and a receiver processes which communicate with each other through the cache footprints left on the L1 cache. For this purpose, the processes had agreed on the meaning of the cache footprint, where each footprint was mapped to either a bit 0, a bit 1 or was invalidated by the receiver. Our attack resembles the attack described in [12], but employed the L1 cache instead of the LLC to covertly transmit information. Similarly to the attack in [12], for sending bit 1, the attacker accesses the whole L1 cache, whereas for sending bit 0 the attacker does not deliberately access the cache. A header and footer are additionally employed to wrap up the transmitted data, so that the receiver could notice where the actual message starts.

The receiver process samples the timestamp counter hardware register (TSC) before and after accessing the cache to be able to infer the cache footprint left by the sender. To enforce executing the instructions in the expected order, we use volatile as a memory barrier, and the CPUID instruction for serialization. The out-of-order execution issue is also considered in [14,17]. Timor et al. apply double execution to protect the out-of-order part of the CPU by executing each instruction twice in [17]. The scheduler's *setaffinity* option is used to request that the sender and the receiver processes will be executed on the same CPU core and will use the same L1 cache.

5.2 Experiments and Results

We conducted 100 experiments per setting, and in each experiment messages of length 5000 were sent over the CC as packets consisting of 1000 bits payload and 500 bits header and footer each. In each experiment the relevant hardware performance counters were logged simultaneously with the attack to enable extracting the feasibility metrics.

Altogether, we have five settings for five different scenarios. The experiments were deployed by simulating load on the system with the stressing tool stress-ng. Background load levels of 0%, 40% and 80% per CPU core were considered in each of the settings with a running attack, and load levels of 40% and 80% were considered for the non-attacked system. As feasibility metrics, we employed the frequency of successive scheduling (SS) between the sender and the receiver, and the times the receiver process is busy waiting (BW). To assess their applicability, we considered the number of successful transmissions (STs) as an indicator for attack's success.

The relationship between the measurements can be seen in Table 1. The results, summarized in the table, demonstrate the large difference between BWs in an attacked and a non-attacked system. This observation is visible also in Fig. 2 showing the tremendous BWs increase in an attacked system compared to a non-attacked system. This confirms that BW can be considered as a starting point for the covert-channel feasibility analysis to focus on a suspicious process. As expected and visible from the results, with the load increase, the STs decrease. This is normal due to more contention for the CC. Indirectly, this is also a scheduling effect, as the scheduler grants all the processes CPU time.

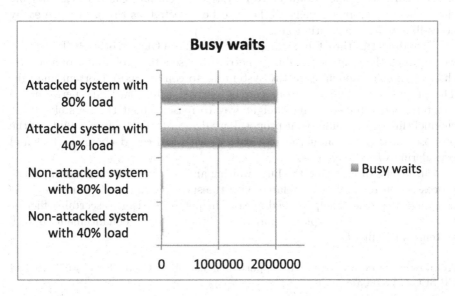

Fig. 2. The bar chart reveals a great difference between the number of BWs in a non-attacked and an attacked system.

Table 1. Results summary.

	CCA employed			No attack	
	0%	40%	80%	40%	80%
# Experiments	100	100	100	100	100
STs (overall)	494007	340735	262599	–	–
STs (average per exp.)	4940.07	3407.35	2625.99	–	–
Standard deviation for ST	305	942	1056	–	–
BW (overall)	2024152	2005113	2016318	4	16
BW (average per exp.)	20241.52	20051.13	20163.18	0.04	0.16

The presented results discern that an increased number of issued BWs can be taken a starting point for the further analysis and, can indicate that measurement of the SSs is needed. The BWs metric is particularly suitable for initiating further investigation due to the minimal performance overhead related to its measurement. By using such an approach, we can have an indicator regarding the probability of a covert-channel exploit.

6 Conclusion

Core-private caches represent a convenient and practical way for exfiltrating secret information and endanger ICT systems, including CIs. Attacks abusing the caches as covert channels are hard to be detected, as the caches are easily accessible without any privileges.

To address this threat and enhance the security in CIs and other ICT systems, we proposed the usage of feasibility metrics to assess the probability of a covert-channel exploit happening in the system or, to conduct post mortem analysis. The proposed feasibility metrics can be derived using hardware performance counters, and represent a lightweight way to reason about the possible covert channel threat. To validate our proposal, we demonstrate the applicability of the proposed metrics by conducting experiments with a L1 covert-channel attack and considering varied scenarios.

Our results discern that the busy waiting and the successive scheduling of the processes can reliably be correlated with the success of a covert-channel exploit using the L1 cache. The proposed metrics help systematically ascertain efficient ways to address such exploits, and to facilitate security enhancement in ICT systems, including CIs.

Acknowledgements. Research supported in part by EC NECS GA#675320 and CIPSEC GA#700378.

References

1. Agrawal, D., Archambeault, B., Rao, J.R., Rohatgi, P.: The EM side—channel(s). In: Kaliski, B.S., Koç, K., Paar, C. (eds.) CHES 2002. LNCS, vol. 2523, pp. 29–45. Springer, Heidelberg (2003). https://doi.org/10.1007/3-540-36400-5_4
2. Gartner, Inc.: Why a No-Cloud Policy Will Become Extinct (2016). https://www.gartner.com/smarterwithgartner/cloud-computing-predicts/. Accessed 10 July 2018
3. Genkin, D., Shamir, A., Tromer, E.: RSA key extraction via low-bandwidth acoustic cryptanalysis. Cryptology ePrint Archive, Report 2013/857 (2013). http://eprint.iacr.org/
4. HIMMS Analytics: 2014 HIMMS Analytics Cloud Survey (2014). https://www.himss.org/file/1308371/download?token=CBkkly5K. Accessed 07 July 2018
5. Hlavacs, H., Treutner, T., Gelas, J.P., Lefevre, L., Orgerie, A.C.: Energy consumption side-channel attack at virtual machines in a cloud. In: Proceedings of the 2011 IEEE International Conference on Dependable, Autonomic and Secure Computing (DASC 2011), pp. 605–612 (2011)

6. Hu, W.M.: Reducing timing channels with fuzzy time. In: Proceedings of the 1991 IEEE Computer Society Symposium on Research in Security and Privacy, pp. 8–20, May 1991

7. Hu, W.M.: Lattice scheduling and covert channels. In: Proceedings of the 1992 IEEE Symposium on Security and Privacy, SP 1992, pp. 52–61. IEEE Computer Society, Washington (1992). http://dl.acm.org/citation.cfm?id=882488.884165

8. Irazoqui, G., Inci, M.S., Eisenbarth, T., Sunar, B.: Wait a minute! A fast, cross-VM attack on AES. In: Stavrou, A., Bos, H., Portokalidis, G. (eds.) RAID 2014. LNCS, vol. 8688, pp. 299–319. Springer, Cham (2014). https://doi.org/10.1007/978-3-319-11379-1_15

9. Kerrisk, M.: The Linux man-pages project (2013). http://man7.org/linux/man-pages/man7/sched.7.html. Accessed 02 July 2018

10. Liu, F., Yarom, Y., Ge, Q., Heiser, G., Lee, R.B.: Last-level cache side-channel attacks are practical. In: Proceedings of the 2015 IEEE Symposium on Security and Privacy, SP 2015, pp. 605–622. IEEE Computer Society, Washington, May 2015

11. Maurice, C., et al.: Hello from the other side: SSH over robust cache covert channels in the cloud. In: Proceedings of the 24th Annual Network and Distributed System Security Symposium, NDSS 2017 (2017)

12. Maurice, C., Neumann, C., Heen, O., Francillon, A.: C5: cross-cores cache covert channel. In: Almgren, M., Gulisano, V., Maggi, F. (eds.) DIMVA 2015. LNCS, vol. 9148, pp. 46–64. Springer, Cham (2015). https://doi.org/10.1007/978-3-319-20550-2_3

13. Maurice, C., Le Scouarnec, N., Neumann, C., Heen, O., Francillon, A.: Reverse engineering intel last-level cache complex addressing using performance counters. In: Bos, H., Monrose, F., Blanc, G. (eds.) RAID 2015. LNCS, vol. 9404, pp. 48–65. Springer, Cham (2015). https://doi.org/10.1007/978-3-319-26362-5_3

14. Mendelson, A., Suri, N.: Designing high-performance and reliable superscalar architectures: the out of order reliable superscalar (O3RS) Approach. In: Proceedings of the International Conference on Dependable Systems and Networks, DSN 2000, pp. 473–481. IEEE Computer Society, June 2000

15. Messerges, T., Dabbish, E., Sloan, R.: Investigations of power analysis attacks on smartcards. In: Proceedings of the USENIX Workshop on Smartcard Technology on USENIX Workshop on Smartcard Technology, WOST 1999, p. 17. USENIX Association, Berkeley (1999)

16. Ristenpart, T., Tromer, E., Shacham, H., Savage, S.: Hey, You, get off of my cloud: exploring information leakage in third-party compute clouds. In: Proceedings of the 16th ACM Conference on Computer and Communications Security, CCS 2009, pp. 199–212. ACM, New York (2009)

17. Timor, A., Mendelson, A., Birk, Y., Suri, N.: Using underutilized CPU resources to enhance its reliability. IEEE Trans. Dependable Secure Comput. 7(1), 94–109 (2010)

18. Varadarajan, V., Ristenpart, T., Swift, M.: Scheduler-based defenses against cross-VM side-channels. In: Proceedings of the 23rd USENIX Security Symposium, USENIX Security 2014, pp. 687–702. USENIX Association, San Diego (2014)

19. Vateva-Gurova, T., Luna, J., Pellegrino, G., Suri, N.: Towards a framework for assessing the feasibility of side-channel attacks in virtualized environments. In: Proceedings of the 11th International Conference on Security and Cryptography - Volume 1: SECRYPT, ICETE 2014, pp. 113–124. SciTePress (2014)

20. Vateva-Gurova, T., Suri, N., Mendelson, A.: The impact of hypervisor scheduling on compromising virtualized environments. In: Proceedings of the 2015 IEEE International Conference on Dependable, Autonomic and Secure Computing, DASC 2015, pp. 1910–1917 (2015)
21. VMware: additional transparent page sharing management capabilities and new default settings. Technical report 2097593, VMware. https://kb.vmware.com/s/article/2097593. Accessed 07 June 2018
22. VMware: security considerations and disallowing inter-virtual machine transparent page sharing. Technical report 2080735, VMware. https://kb.vmware.com/s/article/2080735. Accessed 07 June 2018
23. Xu, Y., Bailey, M., Jahanian, F., Joshi, K., Hiltunen, M., Schlichting, R.: An exploration of L2 cache covert channels in virtualized environments. In: Proceedings of the Workshop on Cloud Computing Security, pp. 29–40 (2011)
24. Yarom, Y., Falkner, K.: FLUSH+RELOAD: a high resolution, low noise, L3 cache side-channel attack. In: Proceedings of the 23rd USENIX Security Symposium, USENIX Security 2014, pp. 719–732. USENIX Association, San Diego (2014)
25. Yarom, Y., Ge, Q., Liu, F., Lee, R.B., Heiser, G.: Mapping the intel last-level cache. IACR Cryptology ePrint Archive 2015, 905 (2015)
26. Zhang, Y., Juels, A., Reiter, M., Ristenpart, T.: Cross-VM side channels and their use to extract private keys. In: Proceedings of the 2012 ACM Conference on Computer and Communications Security, CCS 2012, pp. 305–316. ACM, New York (2012)

Detecting In-vehicle CAN Message Attacks Using Heuristics and RNNs

Shahroz Tariq[1,2], Sangyup Lee[1,2], Huy Kang Kim[3], and Simon S. Woo[1,2(✉)]

[1] Stony Brook University, Stony Brook, NY, USA
{shahroz.tariq,sangyup.lee,simon.woo}@stonybrook.edu
[2] The State University of New York, Korea (SUNY-Korea), Incheon, South Korea
[3] Korea University, Seoul, South Korea
cenda@korea.ac.kr

Abstract. In vehicle communications, due to simplicity and reliability, a Controller Area Network (CAN) bus is used as the de facto standard to provide serial communication between Electronic Control Units (ECUs). However, prior research reveals that several network-level attacks can be performed on the CAN bus due to the lack of underlying security mechanism. In this work, we develop an intrusion detection algorithm to detect DoS, fuzzy, and replay attacks injected in a real vehicle. Our approach uses heuristics as well as Recurrent Neural Networks (RNNs) to detect attacks. We test our algorithm with in-vehicle data samples collected from KIA Soul. Our preliminary results show the high accuracy in detecting different types of attacks.

1 Introduction

The Controller Area Network (CAN) bus [1] is widely used to provide an efficient and economical link between Electronic Control Units (ECUs). The CAN bus is a broadcast-based communication protocol that supports the maximum baud rate up to 1 Mbps on a single bus, developed by Bosch in 1985. CAN bus has been widely adopted because of its small wiring cost, weight, and complexity. However, there are several vulnerabilities that exist in CAN bus, due to its simplicity and efficiency. Because receiving node does not validate the origin of a CAN message, many network traffic injection attacks are possible as shown in other research [8,12]. In particular, Boudguiga et al. [3] discussed the lack of security mechanisms in the CAN protocol which makes it vulnerable to DoS, impersonation, and isolation attacks.

The in-vehicle intrusion detection using the number of messages sent during an interval on CAN bus is discussed in [5,7,9]. Hoppe et al. [6] presented basic attacks from the black box attack on a gateway ECU which enables an attacker to sniff arbitrary internal communications.

Also, Miller et al. [10] showed that they were able to take complete control over the automobile from a remote site by using wireless network, provided

---

S. Tariq and S. Lee—Both authors contributed equally to this work.

© Springer Nature Switzerland AG 2019
A. P. Fournaris et al. (Eds.): IOSec 2018, LNCS 11398, pp. 39–45, 2019.
https://doi.org/10.1007/978-3-030-12085-6_4

the IP address of the vehicle is known. They also demonstrated the degree of control needed for injecting messages onto the CAN bus, and also suggested countermeasures. Müter *et al.* [11] defined the concept of entropy on CAN bus and used it to detect anomalies by associating entropy to a reference set. They also used a more systematized method, which involves sensors to monitor the state of traffic for anomaly detection. Recently, Lee *et al.* [8] discovered that they can detect intrusions with high fidelity by using the response offset ratio and time interval of remote frames. Song *et al.* [12] also used the time intervals of CAN messages. They identified that the time interval between the messages gets changed during the attack state.

In our work, we extend the prior research by providing new capabilities in monitoring, and visualizing real-time attack traffic with higher accuracy in detecting more complex attack patterns using rule-based heuristics as well as Recurrent Neural Networks (RNNs). Our approach is the ensemble of two different detection methods, and complement one another to produce the best detection performance. We evaluate our approach with the samples from CAN datasets collected from KIA Soul [2]. Our preliminary results are highly promising in detecting various types of attacks, and can be integrated into a vehicle as an effective defense mechanism.

2   CAN Bus Threat Models

Attackers can exploit and spoof priority bits in the CAN bus because the single bus is shared by all nodes. In this work, we consider three possible frame injection attacks: (1) DoS Attack, (2) fuzzy attack, and (3) replay attacks. DoS attack can occur if an attacker injects high priority messages in a short cycle on the bus. For example, malicious or infected nodes (devices) can generate DoS attack messages, in order to occupy the CAN bus using the high priority identifier. Since all nodes share a single bus, increasing occupancy on the bus can produce delay or deny arrivals of legitimate messages. Next, fuzzy (or fuzzing) attack can inject messages with randomly spoofed IDs with arbitrary data. In this case, all nodes would receive spoofed aberrant functional messages. To exploit a fuzzy attack, an attacker would first observe and monitor in-vehicle messages and select target IDs to produce unexpected behaviors. The fuzzy attack is typically generated at lower rate than DoS attack. However, it is possible to perform fuzzy attack at higher rate. In a replay attack, an attacker can carefully observe data sequences during a specific time interval, and injects and repeats the whole or part of these legitimate message sequences. Similar to a fuzzy attack, each payload contains a valid CAN control message. The difference between replay and a fuzzy attack is that payloads in a replay attack are not randomly ordered sequences, but they are legitimate repeated-sequences. Hence, detecting a replay attack is more challenging. We will describe how we effectively detect each attack in the next section.

3 Our Approach

Our approach is divided into the following two attack detection methods: (1) heuristics using CAN packet characteristics, and (2) RNNs-based approach. We ensemble the results produced from these detection methods, and determine the final detection.

The heuristics using threshold and signature based approach is shown in Fig. 1. To detect DoS attacks, we focus on capturing packet inter-arrival time features first. Whenever traffic sent at higher rate than normal, we store it into a list of suspicious IDs and we keep monitoring them. If its behavior persists for a certain time duration, we classify it as a DoS Attack.

To detect a fuzzy attack, we maintain a list of last few messages for each node ID (previousList), and calculate the Hamming distance [4] between the new data and data in the previousList. If the Hamming distance is larger than a certain distance, we store this ID into a suspicious ID list. If this behavior persists, we classify it as a fuzzy attack. If the rate of traffic is slower than DoS but it is greater than the average, and two different messages from the same ID are broadcasted on the bus right after another, we store this ID into a list of suspicious IDs. If multiple IDs exhibit similar behaviors and they are persistent for more than a certain time interval, then we can classify them as a replay attack.

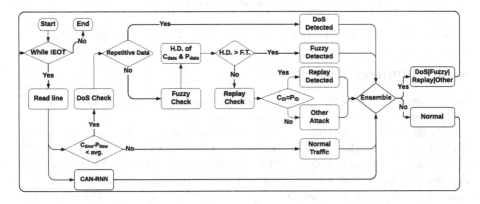

Fig. 1. Intrusion detection algorithm flowchart. Current and previous packets are denoted by C and P, respectively. Time, ID, and Data are the attributes of packet. H.D and F.T stands for Hamming distance and fuzzy threshold respectively.

To overcome possible limitations by above heuristics based detection methods, we train RNNs from CAN dataset for normal, DoS and fuzzy attack traffic. The input sequence to RNNs is a CAN bus packet which is normalized into features. The output is a class label, calculated by probability of being normal traffic as well as each attack type. The first two layers in RNNs are fully connected dense layers with 256 and 512 hidden parameter respectively and a linear rectifier unit (ReLU) is used as an activation function. After each dense layer, we added batch normalization and applied dropout rates of 0.2 and 0.4 respectively. Third and forth layers are LSTMs with 256 hidden cells. Between the two LSTM layers, we added the layer normalization. The final output layer has four classes which can classify from normal, DoS, fuzzy, and replay attacks.

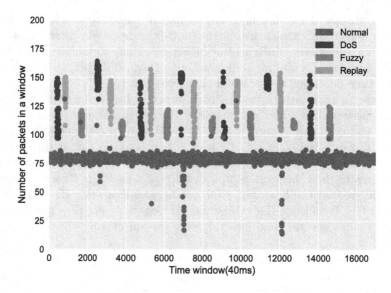

Fig. 2. Real-time visualization of normal & attack traffic (Color figure online)

4   Preliminary Evaluation

In this section, we describe CAN data collection process and provide details on the datasets we used for evaluating our approach.

We used CAN data collected from KIA Soul testing vehicles in [8], where KVASER CAN interface is used to connect CAN bus. Dataset contains 7,504,629 packets in 50 min including 300 DoS and 300 fuzzy attacks. We divided the dataset into two equal sets to train and evaluate RNNs. Figure 2 shows real-time visualization of the classified traffic, where the X-axis represents the time windows, and the Y-axis is number of packets in one window. In Fig. 1, we display all the detect DoS, Fuzzy, and Replay attacks in red, orange, and yellow dots respectively. Furthermore, in Fig. 2, we can display some of traffic not detected as attacks but possible anomalies in a red box as shown in Fig. 2. These CAN packets in Fig. 2 appear to be normal but they are possibly anomalies or new attak types. Following Table 1 shows the precision, recall and F1 of our approach from testing set. We found that our ensemble-based approach achieves high performance with detecting DoS, fuzzy, and replay attack with 99% accuracy. Especially, RNN effectively learned, and performed better for detecting DoS and fuzzy attacks. While heuristic-based approach was better in detecting replay attack. Overall, the final ensemble module improves the overall performance.

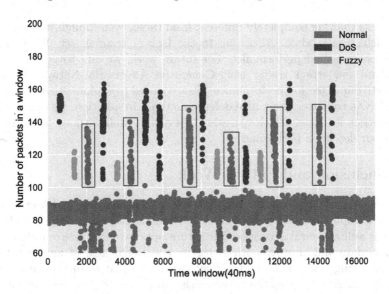

Fig. 3. Anomaly/suspicious behaviors are shown in red boxes. (Color figure online)

Table 1. Overall intrusion attack detection performance using ensembles with test data, where HR and RNN indicates heuristics and RNN only, and E is the ensemble of HR and RNN.

Attack	Precision	Recall	F1
DoS(HR<RNN<E)	99.30%	99.27%	99.29%
Fuzzy(HR<RNN<E)	99.01%	99.35%	99.18%
Replay(RNN<HR<E)	98.69%	99.87%	99.25%

5   Discussion and Limitations

Overall, our algorithm detected all of DoS, fuzzy and replay attacks very well. It demonstrated that our time window based and content inspection methods can detect DoS, fuzzy and replay attacks effectively. In addition, visualization tools help detect and verify actual attack instances. However, we detect some replay attacks a bit early or late for a couple of cases due to varying transmission delay. There is also transmission time delay from an attack source to our algorithm, since the attack packets are not generated from external source instantly. We plan to improve our algorithm to minimize the attack detection start time and the attack detection end time, incorporating transmission delay. Also, we are currently using the Hamming distance to calculate the difference between two data payloads. However, the Hamming distance is sensitive to the size of the data payload. We plan to evaluate different distance metrics in the future (Fig. 3).

In this work, we only consider DoS, fuzzy, and replay attacks, and variations of those. However, it is possible that our approach might not work well with new attacks that are completely different from these, even though we have other attack detection module. Also, due to the lack of training set, RNNs might not achieve expected performance. For future work, we aim to generate more diverse and new attack traffic using Generative Adversarial Networks (GANs) to strength our detection performance. Also, we need to explore other regularization in RNNs to better generalize defense method. In addition, we will consider reinforcement learning, which can work reasonably well without large data to harness our detection performance.

6   Conclusion and Future Work

Our proposed ensemble-based approach shows the effectiveness in detecting DoS, Fuzzy, and Replay attacks by combining the benefits of using network traffic signatures as well as neural networks. The future work is to evaluate our algorithms with more data and improve both heuristics and RNNs against unseen attacks. Beside detecting DoS, Fuzzy, and Replay attacks, we plan to further research on developing an attack mitigation mechanisms to proactively prevent and defend those attacks.

Acknowledgement. We thank anonymous reviews for providing helpful feedback to improve this work. We also thank Korea Internet & Security Agency (KISA) and Korean Institute of Information Security & Cryptology (KIISC) for the release of CAN dataset. This research was supported by the MSIP (Ministry of Science, ICT and Future Planning), Korea, under the "ICT Consilience Creative Program" (IITP-2015-R0346-15-1007) supervised by the IITP (Institute for Information & communications Technology Promotion) and Basic Science Research Program through the NRF of Korea (NRF-2017R1C1B5076474).

References

1. Controller Area Network (CAN bus). https://en.wikipedia.org/wiki/CAN_bus
2. Kia Soul. https://www.kia.com/us/en/vehicle/soul/2018
3. Boudguiga, A., Klaudel, W., Boulanger, A., Chiron, P.: A simple intrusion detection method for controller area network. In: 2016 IEEE International Conference on Communications (ICC), pp. 1–7. IEEE (2016)
4. Hamming, R.W.: Error detecting and error correcting codes. Bell Labs Tech. J. **29**(2), 147–160 (1950)
5. Hoppe, T., Kiltz, S., Dittmann, J.: Security threats to automotive CAN networks – practical examples and selected short-term countermeasures. In: Harrison, M.D., Sujan, M.-A. (eds.) SAFECOMP 2008. LNCS, vol. 5219, pp. 235–248. Springer, Heidelberg (2008). https://doi.org/10.1007/978-3-540-87698-4_21
6. Hoppe, T., Kiltz, S., Dittmann, J.: Automotive IT-security as a challenge: basic attacks from the black box perspective on the example of privacy threats. In: Buth, B., Rabe, G., Seyfarth, T. (eds.) SAFECOMP 2009. LNCS, vol. 5775, pp. 145–158. Springer, Heidelberg (2009). https://doi.org/10.1007/978-3-642-04468-7_13
7. Hoppe, T., Kiltz, S., Dittmann, J.: Security threats to automotive can networks–practical examples and selected short-term countermeasures. Reliab. Eng. Syst. Saf. **96**(1), 11–25 (2011)

8. Lee, H., Jeong, S.H., Kim, H.K.: OTIDS: a novel intrusion detection system for in-vehicle network by using remote frame. In: Privacy, Security and Trust (PST) (2017)
9. Miller, C., Valasek, C.: A survey of remote automotive attack surfaces. Black Hat, USA (2014)
10. Miller, C., Valasek, C.: Remote exploitation of an unaltered passenger vehicle. Black Hat, USA (2015)
11. Müter, M., Asaj, N.: Entropy-based anomaly detection for in-vehicle networks. In: 2011 IEEE Intelligent Vehicles Symposium (IV), pp. 1110–1115. IEEE (2011)
12. Song, H.M., Kim, H.R., Kim, H.K.: Intrusion detection system based on the analysis of time intervals of can messages for in-vehicle network. In: 2016 International Conference on Information Networking (ICOIN), pp. 63–68. IEEE (2016)

CyberSecurity Threats, Assessment and Privacy

A Questionnaire Model for Cybersecurity Maturity Assessment of Critical Infrastructures

Bilge Yigit Ozkan$^{(\boxtimes)}$ (iD) and Marco Spruit (iD)

Department of Information and Computing Sciences, Utrecht University,
Princetonplein 5, 3584 CC Utrecht, Netherlands
{b.yigitozkan, m.r.spruit}@uu.nl

Abstract. Critical infrastructures are important assets for everyday life and wellbeing of the people. People can be effected dramatically if critical infrastructures are vulnerable and not protected against various threats. Given the increasing cybersecurity risks and the large impact that these risks may bring to the critical infrastructures, assessing and improving the cybersecurity capabilities of the service providers and the administrators is crucial for sustainability.

This research aims to provide a questionnaire model for assessing and improving cybersecurity capabilities based on industry standards. Another aim of this research is to provide service providers and the administrators of the critical infrastructures a personalized guidance and an implementation plan for cybersecurity capability improvement.

Keywords: Cybersecurity · Assessment · Capability · Improvement · Critical infrastructure

1 Introduction

It is important to understand the relationship between different security domains. According to ISO 270032 [1], Information security is concerned with the protection of confidentiality, integrity, and availability of information in general, to serve the needs of the applicable information user. Whereas cybersecurity relates to actions that stakeholders should be taking to establish and maintain security in the cyberspace. Cybersecurity relies on information security, application security, network security, and Internet security as fundamental building blocks. The relationships between these security domains are shown in Fig. 1.

Within the cybersecurity and information security domains, there are several subdomains. Subdomains may have different names in different sources but most of the time their scopes are similar. In this research, among the several subdomains of cybersecurity, the *Identity Management and Access Control* subdomain is selected as an example to demonstrate the proposed questionnaire model. Besides being part of the security standards, Identity Management and Access Control is also defined as a category in the Framework for Improving Critical Infrastructure Cybersecurity document published by NIST [2]. Identity Management and Access Control is a security

© Springer Nature Switzerland AG 2019
A. P. Fournaris et al. (Eds.): IOSec 2018, LNCS 11398, pp. 49–60, 2019.
https://doi.org/10.1007/978-3-030-12085-6_5

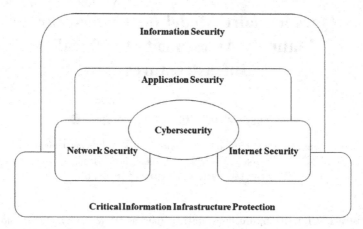

Fig. 1. Relationships between cybersecurity and other security domains (redrawn from ISO/IEC 27032 [1])

discipline comprised of people, processes and technologies to manage identities and access to resources.

Many maturity models have been developed by academics or practitioners to assess domain specific capabilities. In Sect. 2, we give some examples of maturity models including the information security and cybersecurity related ones. These information security and cybersecurity maturity models are complex and comprehensive. They are not easy to implement for self-assessment and, therefore, suitable for preparing customized improvement plans. Another drawback of these information and cybersecurity maturity models is that they do not consider organizational characteristics. These inadequacies led us to our research question: "How can we design a questionnaire to assess and improve cybersecurity capabilities with implementation guidance and taking into account the organizational characteristics?". Based on this research question, we propose a situational-aware questionnaire model for cybersecurity maturity self-assessment of critical infrastructures that also facilitates the generation of a customized improvement plan. The model and its components are described in depth in Sect. 3.

Using the proposed questionnaire based self-assessment model the service providers or administrators of the critical infrastructures can identify areas of improvement and create a plan to improve its cyber security practices, thereby reaching a higher maturity level.

2 Background

2.1 Maturity Models

Maturity Modelling is a method for representing domain specific knowledge in a structured way in order to provide organizations with an evolutionary process for assessment and improvement. Maturity models in different domains have been developed and used mostly since they became popular after the introduction of the

Capability Maturity Model (CMM) of the Software Engineering Institute (SEI) of Carnegie Mellon University [3]. Some maturity model examples for different domains are given in Table 1.

Table 1. Maturity model examples for different domains

Maturity model	Organization/authors
The Smart Grid Maturity Model (SGMM) [4]	CMMI Institute-SEI
Business Process Maturity Model [5]	OMG
People Capability Maturity Model [6]	CMMI Institute-SEI
Test Maturity Model integration (TMMi) [7]	TMMi Foundation

There is an abundance of work related to information security and cybersecurity maturity modelling. Some of these maturity models are given in Table 2.

Table 2. Information and cybersecurity maturity models

Maturity model	Organization/authors
Cybersecurity Capability Maturity Model [8]	US The Department of Energy (DOE)
Open Information Security Management Maturity Model [9]	The Open Group
NICE Cybersecurity Capability Maturity Model [10]	US The Department of Homeland Security
ISFAM (the Information Security Focus Area Maturity Model) [11]	Spruit & Roeling

Spruit and Roeling [11] developed the Information Security Focus Area Maturity Model (ISFAM) which is focused on the information security domain. ISFAM is capable of determining the current information security maturity level and can be used to incrementally and structurally improve information security maturity within the organization. ISFAM is successfully evaluated through several case studies in telecommunications, logistics, healthcare and finance sectors. As the name implies, ISFAM does not focus particularly on cybersecurity related focus areas.

There is no consensus among the maturity models on how to designate the domain specific capability categories. Some of the most common used terms are focus area, process and category. The terms used in the maturity models also depend on the type of the maturity model. In this research, we opted to use the term 'focus area' which is used in the focus area maturity models [12].

2.2   Self-assessment and Required E-Skills for the Questionnaire

As the term implies, self-assessment is a means by which an organization assesses compliance to a selected reference model or module without requiring a formal method [13].

Eventually, the questions included in the questionnaire are domain specific and require cybersecurity domain awareness and skills. The European e-Competence Framework [14] can be used as a reference to understand the required competencies to effectively answer the proposed questionnaire. In the competency area "Manage", the "Information Security Management" competency is the one that matches most of the skills the user of the questionnaire is desired to have.

3   Questionnaire Model

3.1   Components and Their Purposes

In the questionnaire model we have developed, there are nine object types: Focus Area, Question, Standard, Capability, Capability Level, Answer, Action, Training Material/Tip and Task. The relationships between these components are shown in Fig. 2.

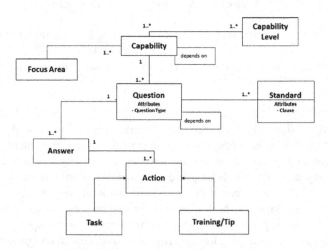

Fig. 2. Relationships between the model components

Focus Area: The sub domains under the cybersecurity security domain such as 'Identity management and access control'.

Question: There are two types of questions: Focus Area Questions and Situational Questions. Focus area questions are the ones questions the cybersecurity capability's implementation. For uniqueness, focus area questions are numbered as F#Q#: Focus

Area Number and Question Number. In this paper, Identity Management and Access Control focus area is selected as an example to demonstrate the model.

The Situational questions are used to identify organizational characteristics for adapting the focus area questions' flow and giving personalized guidance. Situational questions are numbered as SQ#: Situational Question Number.

Standard: Focus area questions are elaborated by investigating different information security and cybersecurity standards. Standards and standard clauses are referenced for the focus area questions.

Capability: The ability to achieve an objective for the focus area. Each focus area consists of a number of different capabilities representing progressive maturity levels.

Capability Level: The level of the organizations capability for a focus area. Questions are prepared to identify different levels of capabilities.

Answer: Possible answers to the questions. Answers are numbered as A#: Answer number.

Action: An action triggered by the answer to a question. Actions can either refer to a Training Material/Tip and/or a Task.

Training Material/Tip: The capability related training or tip that will be displayed to the user for a given answer. Training Materials/Tips are identified as TA#: Training Action Number. The purpose to have training material/tip is to increase the awareness of the organization on the specific capability.

Task: The capability related piece of work that should be done to improve the capability level. Tasks are triggered by answers to a question. Tasks are identified by T#: Task Number. The purpose to have Tasks is to provide organizations an implementation guidance for the specific capability. After scheduling the required tasks and the responsible for implementation, the organization will have an implementation plan for capability improvement for the focus area. The organization will have the opportunity to modify the suggested text for the task.

3.2 Identifying the Focus Area Questions

To be able to use a focus area maturity model as an instrument to assess the current maturity of a functional domain, measures must be defined for each of the capabilities. This can be done by formulating control questions for each capability. These questions can be combined in a questionnaire that can be used in assessments. Formulation of the questions is usually based on the descriptions of the capabilities and on experience and practices [15].

In this research, we have prepared the assessment questions based on ISO 27002 [16] and ETSI TR 103 305 [17] for the 'Identity Management and Access Control' focus area. In Table 3, the referenced standard and the specific clause of the standard can be seen in the third column. Along with the standards, literature can also be used for identifying the capabilities and therefore the focus area questions.

3.3 Identifying the Situational Questions

The situational questions complement the model with a risk analysis perspective that vary by the organizational characteristics. These questions are peculiar to the entity type whose cybersecurity capabilities are being assessed. One of the requirements of establishing an information security management according to ISO 27001 [18] is understanding the organization and its context in order to perform effective risk analysis. The situational questions presented in the model serve the same objective, understanding the organization and its context in order to address the specific requirements of the organization.

An example of a situational question for service providers or administrators of the critical infrastructures can be 'What is the number of people supplied by the Critical Infrastructure?'. The flow of the focus area questions will depend on the answer given to this question. The more people effected by the shutdown of the critical infrastructure, the more complex cybersecurity capabilities are expected to be implemented.

The implementation of more complex cybersecurity capabilities makes the organization more mature in terms of cybersecurity practices. As the number of people supplied by the critical infrastructure increases the impact that a threat may cause also increases hence this increases the risk faced.

Regarding the critical infrastructures, according to Fekete [19], criticality can be described by the following three general characteristics and described as follows:

- Critical proportion: Critical proportion contains aspects such as the critical number of elements or nodes of an infrastructure, choke points, as well as critical number of services, size of population, or magnitude of customers affected.
- Critical time: Critical time summarizes aspects such as duration of outage, speed of onset, and specific critical time frames, but also notes the capacities before, during, and after a crisis.
- Critical quality: Critical quality summarizes aspects such as the quality of the service delivered (for example water quality), and includes public trust in (water) quality.

Since the criticality is directly related to the risks faced by the organization in case of any successful attack, these three characteristics can be used to identify the situational questions for the critical infrastructures. For instance, 'What is the number of people supplied by the Critical Infrastructure?' question is related to 'critical proportion' criterion. In Table 5, other possible situational questions for the critical infrastructures are given as examples.

Different characteristics of an organization/entity should be considered while designing adaptive maturity assessment models. We will further investigate the applicability of the CHOISS model [20] for designing adaptive maturity assessment models.

3.4 The Relationships Between the Model Components

The relationships between the model components are depicted in Fig. 2. Question has the attribute 'Question Type' that can be scale, multiple-choice etc. Standard has an attribute 'Clause' that indicates the specific clause of the relevant standard related to the capability.

4 Questionnaire for Identity Management and Access Control

4.1 Focus Area Questions and Scoring for Capability Implementation

In the questionnaire model, questions are prepared for each capability level (A, B and C). Table 3 shows some example questions selected for the Identity Management and Access Control focus area for each capability level.

In the Prerequisite column, the prerequisite questions or answers can be seen for each of the questions if there is a prerequisite condition for that question. For instance, F1Q3 will only be asked if the answer to F1Q2 is "Yes" (Answer 1). This is an example of intra-focus area dependency i.e. focus area questions depending on the answer for the other questions in the same focus area. The dependency can also be inter-focus area. Another dependency relation may be between the situational questions and the focus area questions. For F1Q5 in Table 3, we see this kind of dependency. F1Q5 is a capability level C question which is the highest level. Designated answers for situational questions in Table 5 show a level of increase with the associated cybersecurity risks. For instance, risk associated with A4 to SQ 2 is higher that the risk associated with A3 and so on. In this perspective, the organization is expected to answer questions that are more complex and intend the higher maturity levels, as their risk is increases. This interpretation also enables the constitution of a personalized capability improvement plan.

In the Action for Answer columns, each specific action defined according to the specific answers can be seen. For instance, If the answer to F1Q1 is "No" (Answer 2) then TA1 and T1 will be triggered.

The focus are questions can be answered as to reflect the implementation ratio of the capability that is being assessed. A question contributes to the scoring only if it has an assigned capability level. Some of the questions are intended to gather additional information from the user or assist the user in some situations in order to increase awareness regarding the capability. These type of questions do not contribute to the scoring. Each question in a capability level contributes to the scoring equally. According to the implementation level that the user chooses, the gathered answer contributes to the score with the percentages given in Table 4. The implementation rating scale used here is adapted from ISO/IEC 15504 standard [21]. Answer # column shows the respective answer options used for the questions in Table 3.

Table 3. An excerpt from the identity management and access control questionnaire

Question number	Question	Standard, clause	Capability level	Question type	Prerequisite question/ answer	Action for answer 1	Action for answer 2	Action for answer 3	Action for answer 4
F1Q1	Do your users login to your systems by unique user-ids?	ISO 27002, 9.2.1.a	A	Scale			TA1, T1	TA1, T1	TA1, T1
F1Q2	Do you periodically review your access rights (including administrator accounts)?	ISO 27002, 9.2.2.f, 9.2.3.f, 9.2.5, ETSI TR 103 305, CSC 16	B	Scale			TA2, T2	TA2, T2	TA2, T2
F1Q3	How frequently do you review your access rights (including administrator accounts)?	ISO 27002, 9.2.5	–	Multiple choice	F1Q2A1				
F1Q4	When have you reviewed your access rights (including administrator accounts) the last time?	–	–	Date/time	F1Q3	T3	T3	T3	T3
F1Q5	Have you enabled audit logging for your administrator accounts?	ISO 27002, 12.4.3	C	Scale	SQ1A2, SQ1A3, SQ1A4, SQ2A2, SQ2A3, SQ2A4 SQ3A2, SQ3A3, SQ3A4, SQ4A1		TA3, T4	TA3, T4	TA3, T4

Table 4. Implementation levels of the capabilities and their contribution percentage to the score

Answer #	Implementation level	% contribution to the score
Answer 1	Fully Implemented (FI)	100
Answer 2	Largely Implemented (LI)	85
Answer 3	Partially Implemented (PI)	50
Answer 4	Not Implemented (NI)	0

4.2 Situational Questions

Examples of the situational questions identified for the critical infrastructures are given in Table 5.

Table 5. An excerpt from the situational questions for critical infrastructures (adopted from [19])

Question number	Question	Question type	Answer 1	Answer 2	Answer 3	Answer 4
SQ1	What is the number of people supplied by the critical infrastructure?	Scale	0– 500.000	500.000– 1 million	1 million– 2 million	More than 2 million
SQ2	What is the mean time to repair, replace, restore the functionality in case of a cyber attack?	Scale	0– 10 min	10 min– 1 h	1–24 h	24 or more hours
SQ3	What is the mean time to react in case of a cyber attack?	Scale	0– 10 min	10 min - 1 h	1–24 h	24 or more hours
SQ4	Does any breakdown in the critical infrastructure impact any other critical infrastructures due to interconnectedness?	Yes/No	Yes	No		

4.3 Training Actions and Tasks for Capability Implementation

In Table 6, the training material and tips are given. Training material can also be videos along with text material. As an example, TA1 has training material to increase

Table 6. Training material and tips for the excerpt questions.

Training material/tip number	Text/video for the training material/tip
TA1	Using unique user IDs enable users to be linked to and held responsible for their actions; the use of group IDs should only be permitted where they are necessary for business or operational reasons, and should be approved and documented
TA2	The review of access rights should consider the following guidelines: • users' access rights should be reviewed at regular intervals, e.g. a period of 6 months, and after any changes, such as promotion, demotion, or termination of employment • user access rights should be reviewed and re-allocated when moving from one employment to another within the same organization; • authorizations for special privileged access rights should be reviewed at more frequent intervals, e.g. at a period of 3 months;
TA3	System administrator and system operator activities should be logged and the logs protected and regularly reviewed

awareness for the usage of unique user-ids. Training material and tips can be compiled from various sources such as standards and literature.

In Table 7, it can be seen that T1 is the task to ensure that all users have unique user-ids. According to the model implementation, user can modify the text for the task and schedule a deadline for it, also assign a responsible.

Table 7. Tasks for the excerpt questions.

Task number	Task definition
T1	Ensure that users login to your systems by unique user-ids
T2	Ensure that access rights (including administrator accounts) are periodically reviewed
T3	Schedule a reminder task for date + the review period
T4	Ensure that audit logging for user accounts (including administrator accounts) is enabled

4.4 Capability Improvement Plan

After answering all the questions, and scheduling the tasks respectively, the organization will have an implementation plan for the capability improvement.

An example capability improvement plan is given in Table 8. In Table 8, we can see the description of the tasks, deadlines for implementation and the responsible persons assigned to the tasks that are scheduled. The tasks for implementing the missing capabilities are grouped by the focus areas. In this capability improvement plan, we can also see the resulting capability score for the focus area. The capability score for the focus area is calculated by accumulating the implementation ratios determined by the user of the assessment questionnaire.

Table 8. An exemplar capability improvement plan

Information security capability improvement plan for UU			
Task number	Description	Deadline	Responsible
Identity management and access control tasks		*Capability score: 50%*	
T1	Ensure that audit logging for user accounts (including administrator accounts) is enabled	01/08/2018	B.Y. Ozkan
Patch management tasks		*Capability score: 35%*	
T1	Ensure that automated patching of the operating system is enabled on all machines	01/07/2018	M.R. Spruit
T2	Ensure that automated patching is enabled for all services and devices interfacing to the internet	01/08/2018	B.Y. Ozkan
T3	Ensure that users do not have the administrator rights on their computers	01/08/2018	B.Y. Ozkan

5 Conclusion

In this research, we have proposed a questionnaire model with various components serving different purposes such as questions for assessing capability, training material for providing awareness, tasks for capability improvement.

The model's implementation with all the components as a whole acts as a potentially useful instrument for self-assessing cybersecurity and improvement planning. The actual application and implementation of the questionnaire model within an organization is beyond the scope of this research. Further research has to be conducted to validate the questionnaire model and to monitor its applicability. Another issue that needs to be addressed in future research is the process of integrating several international or multi-national standards on cybersecurity to compose a coherent set of focus area questions.

In the Horizon2020 SMESEC project, the evaluation of the proposed questionnaire model to assess and improve the cybersecurity capabilities of Small and Medium Sized Enterprises (SMEs) is planned. The focus area questions will remain mainly the same but the situational questions will significantly differ when they are adapted to the characteristics of SMEs.

Acknowledgements. This work was made possible with funding from the European Union's Horizon 2020 research and innovation programme under grant agreement No. 740787 (SMESEC). The opinions expressed and arguments employed herein do not necessarily reflect the official views of the funding body.

References

1. ISO/IEC 27032:2012 - Information technology – Security techniques – Guidelines for cybersecurity. https://www.iso.org/standard/44375.html
2. National Institute of Standards and Technology: Framework for Improving Critical Infrastructure Cybersecurity, Version 1.1. National Institute of Standards and Technology, Gaithersburg, MD (2018)
3. Paulk, M.C., Curtis, B., Chrissis, M.B., Weber, C.V.: Capability Maturity Model, Version 1.1. IEEE Softw. Los Alamitos. **10**, 18–27 (1993). http://dx.doi.org/10.1109/52.219617
4. Smart Grid Maturity Model, Version 1.2: Model Definition. https://resources.sei.cmu.edu/library/asset-view.cfm?assetid=10035
5. About the Business Process Maturity Model Specification Version 1.0. https://www.omg.org/spec/BPMM/
6. People CMM: A Framework for Human Capital Management (SEI Series in Software Engineering Series) | ISBNdb. https://isbndb.com/book/9780321553904
7. TMMi Model. https://www.tmmi.org/tmmi-model/
8. Cybersecurity Capability Maturity Model (C2M2) | Department of Energy. https://www.energy.gov/ceser/activities/cybersecurity-critical-energy-infrastructure/energy-sector-cybersecurity-0-0
9. Open Information Security Management Maturity Model (O-ISM3), Version 2.0. https://publications.opengroup.org/c17b
10. Cybersecurity Capability Maturity Model. https://www.hsdl.org/?view&did=798503

11. Spruit, M., Roeling, M.: ISFAM: the information security focus area maturity model. In: ECIS 2014 Proceedings (2014)
12. van Steenbergen, M., Bos, R., Brinkkemper, S., van de Weerd, I., Bekkers, W.: Improving IS functions step by step: the use of focus area maturity models. Scandinavian J. Inf. Syst. **25**, 2 (2013)
13. Blanchette, S., Keeler, J.K.L.: Self Assessment and the CMMI-AM – A Guide for Government Program Managers, p. 41
14. e-CF overview | European e-Competence Framework. http://www.ecompetences.eu/e-cf-overview/
15. van Steenbergen, M., Bos, R., Brinkkemper, S., van de Weerd, I., Bekkers, W.: The design of focus area maturity models. In: Winter, R., Zhao, J.L., Aier, S. (eds.) DESRIST 2010. LNCS, vol. 6105, pp. 317–332. Springer, Heidelberg (2010). https://doi.org/10.1007/978-3-642-13335-0_22
16. ISO/IEC 27002:2013 - Information technology – Security techniques – Code of practice for information security controls. https://www.iso.org/standard/54533.html
17. ETSI: ETSI TR 103 305 .CYBER; Attribute Based Encryption for Attribute Based Access Control (2018)
18. ISO/IEC 27001:2013 - Information technology – Security techniques – Information security management systems – Requirements. https://www.iso.org/standard/54534.html
19. Fekete, A.: Common criteria for the assessment of critical infrastructures. Int. J. Disaster Risk Sci. **2**, 15–24 (2011). https://doi.org/10.1007/s13753-011-0002-y
20. Mijnhardt, F., Baars, T., Spruit, M.: Organizational characteristics influencing SME information security maturity. J. Comput. Inf. Syst. **56**, 106–115 (2016). https://doi.org/10.1080/08874417.2016.1117369
21. ISO/IEC 15504-2:2003 - Information technology – Process assessment – Part 2: Performing an assessment. https://www.iso.org/standard/37458.html

Threat Modeling the Cloud: An Ontology Based Approach

Salman Manzoor[1]([⊠]), Tsvetoslava Vateva-Gurova[1], Ruben Trapero[2],
and Neeraj Suri[1]

[1] Department of Computer Science, Technische Universität Darmstadt, Darmstadt,
Germany
{salman,vateva,suri}@deeds.informatik.tu-darmstadt.de
[2] Atos Research and Innovation, Madrid, Spain
ruben.trapero@atos.net

Abstract. Critical Infrastructures (CIs) such as e-commerce, energy,
transportation, defense, monitoring etc., form the basis of the modern
ICT society, and these CI's increasingly utilize ICT services such as the
Cloud to provide for scalable, robust and cost-efficient services. Consequently, the resilience of the CI is directly connected with the resilience
of the underlying Cloud infrastructure. However, performing a Cloud
threat analysis (TA) is a challenging task given the complex interconnection of underlying computing and communication services. Thus, the
need is of a comprehensive TA approach that can holistically analyze the
relation across system level requirements and Cloud vulnerabilities.

We target achieving such a requirement based threat analysis by
developing an ontology depicting the relations among actors involved in
the Cloud ecosystem. The ontology comprehensively covers requirement
specifications, interaction among the Cloud services and vulnerabilities
violating the requirements. By mapping the ontology to a design structure matrix, our approach obtains security assessments from varied actor
perspectives. We demonstrate the effectiveness of our approach by assessing the security of OpenStack, an open source Cloud platform, covering
user requirements and services involved in Cloud operations.

1 Introduction

Cloud computing delivers on-demand, scalable and shared resources as "utilities"
on a pay per use basis. This has led to an increased proliferation of the Cloud
in diverse application spaces, and increasingly Critical Infrastructures (CIs) are
utilizing it for its potential for large scale device/sensor/system connectivity,
scalability, high-availability and cost-efficiency. Consequently, as the CIs security becomes dependent on the Cloud's security, the interest to conduct threat
modeling and security evaluation of the Cloud has correspondingly increased
and forms the primary target of this research.

One of the advocated methods for generalized (for Cloud or CI) security
assurance is by performing threat analysis. Threat Analysis (TA) is an approach

© Springer Nature Switzerland AG 2019
A. P. Fournaris et al. (Eds.): IOSec 2018, LNCS 11398, pp. 61–72, 2019.
https://doi.org/10.1007/978-3-030-12085-6_6

to investigate potential attacks that can undermine the security of the system
[16]. However, due to the complex interconnections across the services and also
the diverse functional requirements from the Cloud users[1], the current Cloud
threat analysis approaches typically focus on a particular service or a particular
technology stack [11,17,18,21]. Hence, these schemes lack providing a holistic
view of Cloud security. In addition, the schemes from [13,20] apply very useful
graphical security models (e.g., attack graph/tree), but these suffer from scalability issues limiting their usage for Cloud based systems.

To address the aforementioned limitations, a comprehensive threat analysis
approach is desired that can analyze the (a) relationship across different actors
involved in the Cloud ecosystem, and (b) requirements and threats stemming
from the violation of the requirements. Consequently, our research contributions
address two main facets. First, we develop an ontology capturing the Cloud
actors and relationship among the actors. The actors involved in the ontology
are requirements, threats/vulnerabilities and Cloud services. For Cloud services,
we consider OpenStack [15], a popular open source Cloud environment to infer
the services and their interaction in performing fundamental operations such as
launching a Virtual Machine (VM) on behalf of the user. Secondly, the paper
models and investigates security threats from varied perspectives of the Cloud
actors. For this purpose, we map the ontology to a Design Structure Matrix
(DSM) [2]. Among the advantages of the DSM are scalability and applicability
of different algorithms (e.g., clustering, sequencing and tearing) to perform a
comprehensive threat analysis.

On this background, the specific contributions of this paper are as follows.

1. The development of an ontology based approach to identify the relation
   between the actors involved in the Cloud ecosystem.
2. The development of a threat analysis approach utilizing the Design Structure
   Matrix (DSM) to analyze threats to/from Cloud actors.

The remainder of the paper is organized as follows. Section 2 reviews contemporary threat analysis approaches for the Cloud. In Sect. 3 we detail the insights
of the proposed ontology and perform threat analysis using design structure
matrix while, Sect. 4 illustrates a case study on the effectiveness of the proposed
approach for analyzing threats in OpenStack.

2   Related Work

Threat analysis enables the systematic identification of threats that can potentially undermine a system. The initial efforts in threat modeling and analysis,
albeit at the software level, were led by Microsoft to develop STRIDE [4], a
threat modeling approach applicable to data flow diagrams having the potential to explore threats in the system. In schemes [5,6], Hiller et al. identify
propagation of the data errors and their flow in the software. They introduced

---

[1] At a semantic level, a CI is an instantiation of a user.

the concept of error permeability to measure the process of exploring software vulnerability to find software modules that have higher a significance for error propagation across the Software. Their analysis also explore suitable locations for error detection and recovery mechanisms. The scheme presented in [20] developed an attack tree of the Cloud to explore paths that an attacker can use to undermine the security of the Cloud. The authors used a high level abstraction of the Cloud services and even for such a model the scalability of the attack tree suffers. Threat analysis approaches that focus on a particular technology include [14,17]. In [14], authors performed analysis to classify different types of threats impacting the security of the hypervisor/virtualization layer. They classified threats considering their consequence on the functionality of the hypervisor. Therefore, the threats were classified with respect to different functions of the hypervisor such as virtual CPUs management, symmetric multiprocessing, soft memory management unit, etc. Complementing this classification, authors in [17] explored security issues that could incur over VM hopping, VM mobility and VM diversity. Their assessment comprehensively covered the security threats in the virtualization layer across different Cloud deployments. In [7], the authors proposed vulcan, a vulnerability assessment framework for the Cloud. The framework developed an ontology knowledge base by extracting information from vulnerability reports published in the national vulnerability database [1]. Although, they developed a general ontology though the lack of detailed specification of the Cloud model limits the effective application of their ontology framework. In a similar vein, the authors in [19] proposed an ontology for the vulnerability management. The developed the relation between different components involved in successfully exploiting the vulnerability existing in the system. They considered a single perspective of the ontology, i.e., the relationships in the ontology were aligned towards the attacker and his/her objective of exploiting the system. Thus, the relation among the services and requirements were limited in their ontology.

Our work differs from the existing approaches in that we (a) systematically explore the multi-dimensional relations between the different actors involved in the Cloud ecosystem, and (b) perform threat analysis with respect to the relations and constraints among the actors of the Cloud.

3   Requirements Based Threat Analysis

In order to perform requirements based threat modeling of the Cloud, we develop an ontology depicting the relationships across the different actors involved in the ontology. The primary high-level actors being the abstract user, the Cloud and the threats as shown in Fig. 1. In the following sections, we explain the ontology from the perspective of these actors i.e., the constraints and relations across the user, the Cloud and the threats/vulnerabilities followed by mapping the ontology to the DSM for threat analysis.

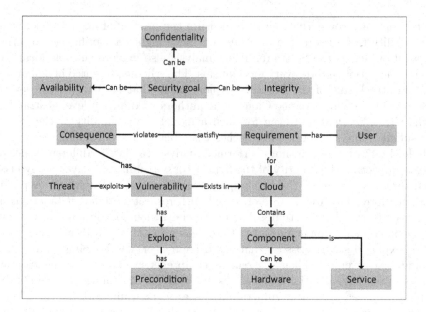

Fig. 1. Correlation among services, requirements and threats

3.1 User and Requirement Capturing

This section captures the requirements of the user. The user specifies his/her requirements for the Cloud and assign weights to each requirement indicating its critically. These weights are qualitatively assigned using linguistic terms such as Highly-Critical (HC), Critical (C), Less-Critical (LC) and Not-Critical (NC). The HC requirements are more important to the user, and therefore, violation of HC requirements or threats compromising these requirements have higher significance than the critical, less-critical and not-critical requirements. As depicted in Fig. 1, the requirement satisfies a specific security goal which could be maintaining Confidentiality (C), Integrity (I) and Availability (A).

3.2 Cloud Perspective of the Ontology

The Cloud is an important actor in the ontology and the user requirements describes his/her preference driving the Cloud usage. As shown in Fig. 1, the Cloud contains different components including hardware and services that it offers to the user. The ontology offers a minimalistic representation of the Cloud. However, to evaluate the possible violation of the requirement across different services or multi-stage threats, a Cloud model depicting the relation between services is needed. Therefore, in Fig. 2, we show essential services in the Cloud and their interactions in launching a Virtual Machine (VM). In order to create this model, we surveyed multiple open source Cloud computing platforms such as [10,12,15] and abstracted their essential services to create the model representing the Cloud operations.

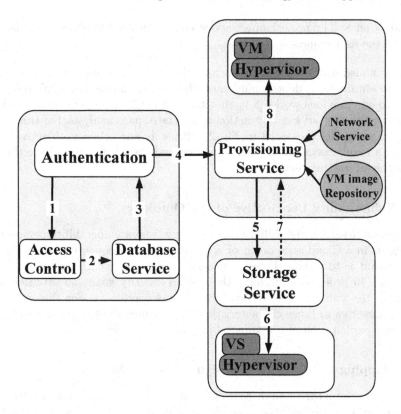

Fig. 2. Services and their interaction in the Cloud

The illustration of service relationships is essential in evaluating the violation of the requirement and propagation of the respective threat across the interacting services. The services interactions of Fig. 2 are described in the following.

- Transitions 1, 2, and 3: These transitions are responsible for performing authentication and validation of the access roles of the user. This prevents the user from accessing/utilizing the resources of other tenants residing in the same physical machine.
- Transition 4: After validating user credentials the user can request provisioning service to initiate a new Virtual Machine (VM) or perform various operations on the existing user's VM. These set of operations include restarting a VM, pausing a VM, etc.
- Transition 5, 6, and 7: The storage service is responsible for providing virtual storage options to the user's VM. For completeness, we have included network service and repository service in the model as these services respectively perform tasks related to network operations (such as assigning virtual network interface, mapping between the virtual and physical network interfaces, etc.) and managing repository of the operating system images that can be readily used by the user for their VMs.

– Transition 8: The provisioning service communicates with the hypervisor to fulfill the user request.

We can also utilize techniques such as the state space analysis of the Cloud model to obtain an in depth analysis on the services interactions. We refer the reader to our previous works [8,9] that target the Cloud's operational services, and also detail the services interaction using state space analysis. For this work, the abstract model presented in Fig. 2 suffices as our primary objective is to perform a requirement based threat analysis and the implication of the threats across the interacting services.

3.3   Vulnerability Perspective of the Ontology

This section describes the utility of an ontology from a vulnerability perspective that exists in a Cloud component or a service. The consequence of the vulnerability exploit is to violate the security goals and cause damage to the user and the Cloud. In order to undermine the system security goals, an attacker tries to exploit the vulnerability by satisfying its pre-conditions. For this work, we restrict ourselves to these characteristics of the vulnerability without exploring the actual exploitation of the vulnerability by the attacker.

3.4   Mapping Ontology to a Design Structure Matrix

In order to perform threat analysis from the perspectives of varied actors, we map the ontology to a Design Structure Matrix (DSM). A DSM offers visualization advantage in illustrating the relations among entities by marking the respective rows and columns. Furthermore, the advantages of a DSM include multi-facet representation and reordering of a DSM to a particular perspective [3]. Thus, the DSM provides a coherent visualization of the ontology and the relationships across the actors and allows restructuring for profiling varied actors. Therefore, in Fig. 3, we show the mapping of the ontology, consisting of requirements, services and vulnerabilities as the primary actors and their relationships, to a DSM.

		Requirements			Services			Vulnerabilities		
#		R 1	R 2	R 3	S 1	S 2	S3	V 1	V2	V3
1	R 1				X			X		
2	R 2					X			X	
3	R 3		X				X		X	X
4	S 1	X					X			
5	S 2		X							
6	S 3	X		X						
7	V 1	X			X					
8	V 2		X	X		X				
9	V 3			X			X			

Fig. 3. Interactions among actors of the ontology

Row# 1 in Fig. 3 exhibits the relation (marked as X) between requirement $R1$, service $S1$ and vulnerability $V1$. The requirement applies to the service $S1$ and the potential vulnerability $V1$ can be used to violate the requirement by exploiting it on $S1$ and thus, undermining the security goal of $R1$. The DSM can also maintain a transitive relation, for example, row# 4 identifies a transitive relation between $R1$ and $S3$ through service $S1$. Furthermore, the interaction between $S1$ and $S3$ could be utilized in launching a multi-stage attack. Similarly, a requirement can depend on other requirement for its proper functionality. This is shown in row# 3 where requirement $R3$ depends on $R2$ and in case of $R3$ violation, the functionality of $R2$ could also suffer.

The DSM also offers varied options for partitioning and restructuring its data elements as a means of exploring inter-relations. For example, we can restructure the DSM to identify the highest influential actor, i.e., the actor with the highest dependencies or interactions. We can achieve this by reordering the DSM rows and columns to transform the DSM to a matrix that has the highest dependency/interactions at the first row and the least dependent/interactions is placed at the last row. This is achieved using the following two steps:

- Step 1: Actors with highest number of dependencies/interactions have maximum number of values (marked as X) in their respective columns and thus, placed at the top of the DSM.
- Step 2: Actors that are ad-hoc and do not provide information on other actors are placed at the bottom of the DSM. This can be identified by observing the empty columns in the DSM.

Applying these two steps to Fig. 3 recursively reorders the DSM with actors having highest dependency/interactions placed at row number 1. This reordered DSM is shown in Fig. 4 which shows that requirement $R3$ has the highest number of dependency/interaction among the actors. Thus, the requirement $R3$ is the most influential while the service $S2$ has the least influence on other actors involved in the ontology.

	R3	V2	R1	R2	S1	S3	V1	V3	S2
R3		X		X		X		X	
V2	X			X					X
R1					X		X		
R2		X							X
S1		X				X			
S3	X		X						
V1	X				X				
V3	X					X			
S2				X					

Fig. 4. Most influential actors

The advantages of such an analysis are to prioritize the vulnerability and calculate the cost of patching the vulnerability. For example, a vulnerability affecting a highly critical requirement should have the highest priority for the patch. Alternatively, the most influential actor can be used to assess the impact of the vulnerability holistically and the system administrator can accordingly calculate the associated risk of the vulnerability.

4   Case Study: Profiling Security of the Cloud

In this section, we elaborate, using a case study, the effectiveness of the proposed ontology and DSM-based approach for profiling Cloud threats from varied perspectives of the involved actors. Table 1 presents an excerpt of the data from the actors that is used to assess the threats holistically considering the relationship among the actors. The requirements field in the table describes the user requirement, its goal and the respective priority assigned by the user. The goal indicates the security purpose of the requirement while, vulnerabilities are exploited by the attacker to undermine this security goal.

Table 1. Excerpt of the actors data for profiling threats in the Cloud

Requirements				Threats			Cloud services		
ID	Description	Priority	Goal	ID	Impact	Description	Name (ID)	Function-ality	Interco-nnection
R1	Each user should have a unique user name and password to utilize Cloud services	HC	CIA	V1	CI	Incorrect timestamps comparison for tokens leads to retaining access via an expired token	Keystone (S1)	Identity and Access Manage-ment	Database Service (S2)
R2	The data at rest should be encrypted and only the authorized user should be able to decrypt	C	A	V2	I	Improper client connections handling leads to denial of service	Keystone (S1)	Identity and Access Manage-ment	Storage (S3)
R3	The data in transfer should be encrypted	C	C	V3	A	Changing the device owner of the port leads to bypassing IP anti-spoofing controls	Neutron (S4)	Network related operations	Hypervisor (S5)
R4	The Cloud service providers should not be able to delete, modify or access user's data	HC	CIA	V4	CIA	When using Xen as a hypervisor, attackers can obtain sensitive password information by reading log files	Hypervisor (S5)	Virtualiza-tion Manage-ment	Keystone, Storage

The vulnerabilities presented in the table are extracted from publicly available database, e.g., NIST's national vulnerability database [1]. The database discloses every vulnerability, its impact and affected products to the public. The Cloud services presented in the table are extracted from the model (cf., Sect. 3.2). However, we map the respective services of the model to the actual OpenStack service name. Thus, the name field in Table 1 represents the corresponding OpenStack service name performing the designated functionality. For example, *Keystone* service in OpenStack is responsible for identity and access management. The relations among requirements, threats and services are also indicated in the table. For example, the requirement $R1$ serves multiple security purposes (CIA) for the user while, the associated threat delineate CI of the security purposes by exploiting the vulnerability on the responsible service $S1$. To comprehensively cover different aspects of the threat assessment, we create a DSM, shown in Fig. 5, using the data of Table 1. The relationship among the Cloud actors is represented in the DSM by marking X in the respective row and column. For completeness, we included *goal* and *priority* for identifying threats violating a specific goal or assessing influence of the requirement in the Cloud. In the following section, we utilize reordering and restructuring of the DSM to assess influence of different actors in the Cloud.

	Requirements				Priority			Goal			Cloud Services					Vulnerabilities			
	R1	R2	R3	R4	HC	C	LC	C	I	A	S1	S2	S3	S4	S5	V1	V2	V3	V4
R1	▓				X			X	X	X	X					X			
R2		▓				X			X	X	X		X				X		
R3			▓			X		X						X				X	
R4				▓	X			X	X	X					X				X
HC	X			X	▓														
C		X	X			▓													
LC							▓												
C	X							▓								X			
I	X								▓								X		
A	X	X								▓									
S1	X	X									▓	X	X			X	X		
S2											X	▓							
S3											X		▓						
S4			X											▓				X	
S5											X		X		▓				X
V1	X							X	X		X					▓			
V2		X							X		X						▓		
V3			X							X				X				▓	
V4				X				X	X	X					X				▓

Fig. 5. Design structure matrix of the case study data

4.1 Extracting Influential Actors Using DSM

We now illustrate how reordering the DSM (steps from Sect. 3.4) can help identify the most influential actor. We rearrange the DSM by placing the most interconnected element, marked as X, to the first row and recursively perform this operation. The rearranged DSM is shown in Fig. 6 having the most influential actor at the first row. The most influential component is requirement $R1$ a highly critical requirement for the user and also the most influential due to its interactions with most of the actors involved. Thus, violating this requirement or vulnerability affecting this requirement has the potential to propagate across the system due to its high degree of connections. Alternatively, from the threat analysis perspective, the DSM identifies critical aspects of the threat propagation and impact on the system. For example, vulnerability $V1$ can be used to undermine $R1$ by compromising service $S1$. However, $S1$ can also be compromised by vulnerability $V2$ and due to $S1$ interactions with services $S2$ and $S3$, the likelihood of propagation of threats should also be assessed. The DSM can also be used to lower the number of dependencies to restrict the impact of the respective actor. On the contrary, we can also examine the least influential actor using bottom-up approach in Fig. 6.

	R1	R4	S1	R2	V4	R3	V1	V2	V3	S5	HC	C	C	I	A	S4	S2	S3	LC
R1	■		X			X						X		X	X				
R4		■			X						X	X		X	X				
S1	X		■	X		X	X										X	X	
R2			X	■				X				X			X				
V4		X			■						X	X	X	X	X				
R3						■			X			X	X		X				
V1	X		X				■					X	X						
V2			X	X				■							X				
V3				X	X				■							X			
S5			X	X						■								X	
HC	X	X									■								
C			X			X						■							
C	X						X						■						
I	X								X					■					
A	X			X											■				
S4						X			X							■			
S2			X														■		
S3										X								■	
LC																			■

Fig. 6. Reordering to extract most influential actor.

Alternatively we can tear the DSM to analyze it from a specific perspective. For example, Fig. 7 shows the perspective of tearing the DSM for analyzing threats that impact confidentiality of the system. As the figure depicts, the critical vulnerability to undermine confidentiality is $V1$ which is exploited on service $S1$. Similarly, $V1$ can be used to undermine the requirements $R1$ and $R2$. Therefore, $V1$ patching should be prioritized in order to maintain the confidentiality of the system.

Beside these two facets, we cam also reorder DSM to identify services exposed to most vulnerabilities. Similarly, the reordering can be utilized to extract threats stemming from a particular requirement.

	C	V1	S1	R1	R2	R3	R4	S4	S5
C		X				X	X		
V1	X		X	X	X				
S1									
R1									
R2									
R3	X							X	
R4	X								X
S4						X			
S5							X		

Fig. 7. From the view point of confidentiality

5   Conclusions and Future Work

In this paper, we have explored the relation among different actors involved in the Cloud ecosystem to develop an ontology. This ontology is further mapped to a design structure matrix for evaluating threats from varied actors perspectives. Our DSM-based threat analysis can be utilized to identify the most critical/influential as well as least critical/influential actor in the Cloud. However, our DSM-based approach is flexible and thus, it can be used to reveal other critical information such as classifying vulnerabilities that achieve a common goal. We believe that by systematically identifying the Cloud vulnerabilities, the CI based on using the Cloud can consequentially be better protected.

In our future work, we will focus on improving the ontology by including countermeasures, composite vulnerabilities and more refined pre-conditions of the vulnerabilities. We will comprehensively perform threat assessment by applying different algorithms to the DSM. These algorithms include sequencing that can be used to illustrate interactions among the vulnerabilities and their propagation and tearing to limit the DSM structure to a point of interest for exploring a particular pattern/set of vulnerabilities presence in the system.

Acknowledgments. Research supported in part by grants NECS GA# 675320 and CIPSEC GA# 700378.

References

1. NIST. National Vulnerability Database. https://nvd.nist.gov/
2. Eppinger, S., Browning, T.: Design Structure Matrix Methods and Applications. MIT Press, Cambridge (2012)
3. Gebala, D., Eppinger, S.: Methods for analyzing design procedures. In: Proceedings of Design Theory and Methodology, pp. 227–233 (1991)
4. Hernan, S., Lambert, S., Ostwald, T., Shostack, A.: Uncover security design flaws using the STRIDE approach. MSDN Magazine (2006)
5. Hiller, M., Jhumka, A., Suri, N.: An approach for analysing the propagation of data errors in software. In: International Conference on Dependable Systems and Networks, DSN 2001, pp. 161–170. IEEE (2001)

6. Hiller, M., Jhumka, A., Suri, N.: EPIC: profiling the propagation and effect of data errors in software. IEEE Trans. Comput. **53**(5), 512–530 (2004)
7. Kamongi, P., et al.: VULCAN: vulnerability assessment framework for cloud computing. In: Proceedings of IEEE Software Security and Reliability (SERE), pp. 218–226 (2013)
8. Manzoor, S., Luna, J., Suri, N.: AttackDive: diving deep into the cloud ecosystem to explore attack surfaces. In: Proceedings of IEEE Services Computing (SCC), pp. 499–502 (2017)
9. Manzoor, S., Taha, A., Suri, N.: Trust validation of cloud IaaS: a customer-centric approach. In: Proceedings of IEEE Conference on Trust, Security and Privacy in Computing and Communications (Trustcom), pp. 97–104 (2016)
10. Milojičić, D., Llorente, I., Montero, R.: Opennebula: a cloud management tool. IEEE Internet Comput. **15**, 11–14 (2011)
11. Myagmar, S., Lee, A., Yurcik, W.: Threat modeling as a basis for security requirements. In: Symposium on Requirements Engineering for Information Security (SREIS), pp. 1–8 (2005)
12. Nurmi, D., et al.: The eucalyptus open-source cloud-computing system. In: Proceedings of Cluster Computing and the Grid (CCGRID), pp. 124–131 (2009)
13. Oladimeji, E., Supakkul, S., Chung, L.: Security threat modeling and analysis: a goal-oriented approach. In: Proceedings of IEEE International Conference on Software Engineering and Applications (IASTED), pp. 13–15 (2006)
14. Perez-Botero, D., et al.: Characterizing hypervisor vulnerabilities in cloud computing servers. In: Proceedings of the International Workshop on Security in Cloud Computing, pp. 3–10 (2013)
15. Sefraoui, O., Aissaoui, M., Eleuldj, M.: OpenStack: toward an open-source solution for cloud computing. Int. J. Comput. Appl. **55**, 38–42 (2012)
16. Swiderski, F., Snyder, W.: Threat Modeling. Microsoft Press (2004)
17. Tsai, H., et al.: Threat as a service?: virtualization's impact on cloud security. IT Prof. **14**, 32–37 (2012)
18. Walter, C.J., Suri, N., Hugue, M.M.: Continual on-line diagnosis of hybrid faults. In: Cristian, F., Le Lann, G., Lunt, T. (eds.) Dependable Computing for Critical Applications 4. DEPENDABLECOMP, vol. 9, pp. 233–249. Springer, Vienna (1995). https://doi.org/10.1007/978-3-7091-9396-9_21
19. Wang, J.A., Guo, M.: Security data mining in an ontology for vulnerability management. In: Proceedings of IEEE Bioinformatics, Systems Biology and Intelligent Computing (IJCBS), pp. 597–603 (2009)
20. Wang, P., Lin, W.-H., Kuo, P.-T., Lin, H.-T., Wang, T.C.: Threat risk analysis for cloud security based on attack-defense trees. In: Proceedings of Computing Technology and Information Management (ICCM), pp. 106–111 (2012)
21. Winter, S., Sârbu, C., Suri, N., Murphy, B.: The impact of fault models on software robustness evaluations. In: Proceedings of International Conference on Software Engineering (ICSE), pp. 51–60 (2011)

Automated Measurements
of Cross-Device Tracking

Konstantinos Solomos[1]($\boxtimes$), Panagiotis Ilia[1], Sotiris Ioannidis[1],
and Nicolas Kourtellis[2]

[1] FORTH, Heraklion, Greece
{solomos,pilia,sotiris}@ics.forth.gr
[2] Telefonica Research, Barcelona, Spain
nicolas.kourtellis@telefonica.com

Abstract. Although digital advertising fuels much of today's free Web,
it typically do so at the cost of online users' privacy, due to continuous
tracking and leakage of users' personal data. In search for new ways to
optimize effectiveness of ads, advertisers have introduced new paradigms
such as cross-device tracking (CDT), to monitor users' browsing on multiple screens, and deliver (re)targeted ads in the appropriate screen.
Unfortunately, this practice comes with even more privacy concerns for
the end-user. In this work, we design a methodology for triggering CDT
by emulating realistic browsing activity of end-users, and then detecting
and measuring it by leveraging advanced machine learning tools.

1 Cross-Device Tracking: An Imminent Privacy Problem

Online advertising can be easily tailored to the audience, to become personalized
to each particular user according to her needs and interests. Until recently, ad-
companies would typically target each user with ads according to the behavior on
a specific device. However, since users own multiple devices, advertisers started
moving towards more advanced targeting practices that are designed to track
users across their devices, and target users regardless of the device used.

According to a recent FTC Report [1], Cross-Device Tracking (CDT) can be
deterministic, where first-party login services (e.g., Facebook, Gmail) that can
track users across devices are being used, or probabilistic, where there are no
shared identifiers between devices, and third parties try to identify which devices
belong to the same user by considering network access data and patterns in
browsing history and behavior etc. Ad-companies that engage in CDT typically
use a mixture of both techniques, but in either case, the implications for user
privacy are severe: they are capable of tracking users across all their digital space,
and use such information in a non-transparent fashion.

It is inherently difficult to detect and measure probabilistic cross-device tracking in a systematic way, as it is heavily based on user activity. Therefore, recent
privacy regulations (e.g., EU's GDPR and ePrivacy) will not be easy to enforce
in such cases. The main problem in measuring CDT lies in distinguishing which

A. P. Fournaris et al. (Eds.): IOSec 2018, LNCS 11398, pp. 73–80, 2019.
https://doi.org/10.1007/978-3-030-12085-6_7

ads are presented to the user because of her behavior on a device (targeting or retargeting), and which ads are because of her activity on a different device.

A few recent works investigated CDT based on technologies such as ultrasound and Bluetooth, and measured the prevalence of these approaches [2,3]. A work by Brookman et al. [4], one of the few that investigate CDT on the web, provides some initial insights about the prevalence of trackers. It examines 100 popular websites in order to determine which of them disclose data to trackers and identifies which websites contain trackers known to employ CDT techniques. Zimmeck et al. [5] designed an algorithm that estimates similarities and correlates the devices into pairs, based on IP addresses and browsing history. That approach shows that users' network information and browsing history can be used for pairing user devices, and thus potentially for CDT.

Our work builds on these early studies on CDT and also on past studies on the detection of web tracking during targeted ads. We propose a first of its kind methodology for the systematic investigation of probabilistic CDT, by leveraging artificially-created behavioral profiles, and measuring the factors affecting CDT in various experimental setups. The contributions of this work are as follows:

- A methodology for detecting CDT based on triggering behavioral cross-device targeted ads on one user device, according to a specific emulated browsing behavior, and then detecting these ads when delivered on a different device.
- An investigation of the factors that affect the performance of CDT under different experimental configurations. We establish artificially-created behavioral profiles with specific web behaviors, and measure the existence of CDT.

2   Methodology to Measure CDT

The main goal of this work is to design a concrete methodology for measuring cross-device tracking activity, as well as to identify the dominant factors that affect the performance of CDT. The methodology emulates realistic browsing activity of end-users with specific web interests across different devices, and collects and analyzes all ads delivered to these devices, due to static advertising or targeted, behavioral or retargeted advertising. Finally, it compares these ads with baseline browsing activity to establish if cross-device tracking is present or not, at what level, its lifetime, and for which types of user interests.

The design of this methodology focuses on the following design objectives:

- Ability to detect probabilistic CDT in a systematic and repeatable fashion.
- Scalability, for fast deployment of multiple parallel device instances, for increased data collection.
- Support the investigation of cross-device tracking in both directions, i.e., mobile → desktop, and desktop → mobile.
- Employ advanced machine learning analysis to compute probability of cross-device tracking in a given experimental setup.
- Support short and long-term experiments, for data collection in ad-hoc fashion or historically through time, respectively.

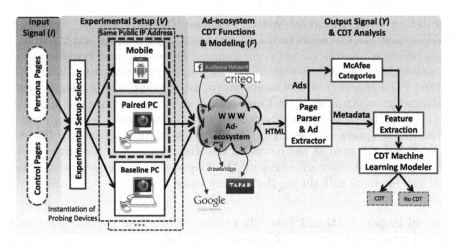

Fig. 1. High level representation of methodology design principles and units.

2.1 Design Principle

In general, we consider the cross-device tracking performed by the ad-ecosystem as a complex process, with multiple parties involved, and not easy to dissect and understand. To infer its internal mechanics we rely on probing this ecosystem with consistent and repeatable inputs $(\mathcal{I})$, under specific experimental settings $(\mathcal{V})$, allow the ecosystem to process and use this input via transformations and modeling $(\mathcal{F})$, and produce measurable outputs on the receiving end $(\mathcal{Y})$:

$$(\mathcal{I}, \mathcal{V}) \xrightarrow{\mathcal{F}} \mathcal{Y}$$

Following this design principle, our methodology allows researchers to push realistic input signals to the ad-ecosystem via website visits, and measure the ad-ecosystem's output through the delivered ads, to demonstrate if $\mathcal{F}$ has allowed or not the ad-ecosystem to perform probabilistic CDT. Based on this design principle an overview of our methodology is illustrated in Fig. 1.

2.2 Methodology Challenges and Considerations

Devices and IPs. The approach we follow is based on triggering and identifying cross-device targeted ads, specifically ads that appear on one of the user's devices but have been triggered by the user's activity on a different device. Our methodology requires a minimum of three different devices (as seen in Fig. 1): one mobile device and two desktop computers, as well as two different IPs. We assume that two of these devices (i.e., the mobile and one desktop) belong to the same user and are connected to the same network. The second desktop (i.e., *baseline PC*), which has a different IP address, is used for receiving a different flow of ads while replicating the browsing of the user's desktop (i.e., *paired PC*). This control instance is used for establishing a baseline set of ads to compare with the ads received by the paired PC.

Emulating User Behavior with Personas: Training Phase. To trigger CDT, we first need to input to the ad-ecosystem some network activity from a user's browsing behavior ($\mathcal{I}$). In order to make the methodology systematic and repeatable, but also produce realistic browsing traffic from scripted browsers, the method visits specific websites to emulate a user's behavior according to some predefined *personas*, similarly to Carrascosa et al. [6]. We leverage this approach for emulating browsing behavior according to specific user interests (e.g., travel and vacations, sports, shopping, etc.), and to create multiple personas of different granularities. For each of the personas, the methodology can identify a set of websites that have active ad campaigns (*training pages*), which the given persona visits and interacts with during the *training* phase.

Control Pages: Testing Phase. To reduce any bias from possible behavioral ads delivered to specific type of websites, the desktops collect ads by visiting *control pages*, i.e., neutral websites (weather, news) that typically serve ads not related to their content. During the testing phase, each device visits the control pages, and the method extracts, analyzes and categorizes the collected ads, in order to identify those ads that have been served to the user's desktop computer because of the browsing behavior on the mobile device.

CDT Detection: Comparing Signals. In order to detect CDT, various statistical methods can be used to associate the input signal $\mathcal{I}$ of persona browsing in the mobile device, with the output signal $\mathcal{Y}$ of ads delivered to the desktop. For example, methods that perform similarity computation between the two signals in a given dimensionality (e.g., Jaccard, Cosine) can be of use. However, since the ad distribution techniques used by the ad-ecosystem are still unknown, we can employ advanced methods, such as machine learning techniques, for the classification of the signals as similar enough to match, or not, based on specific features from the experimental setup ($\mathcal{V}$), and the input/output features. In this methodology we opt for typical methods of machine learning, to compute the likelihood of the two signals being the product of CDT.

3 Measuring CDT in the Wild

This section describes the operational settings of our methodology during the experiments conducted for measuring CDT and its effect on the ad-ecosystem.

3.1 Experimental Setup

Personas and Training Pages. A critical part of the methodology is the design and automatic building of realistic user personas. Each persona has a unique collection of visiting websites that form the set of *persona pages*. Since we do not know in advance which e-commerce sites are conducting cross-device campaigns, our personas must cover a wide area of interests. For this reason, we

Table 1. Behavioral personas generated for emulating user browsing activity.

Persona	Category - Description
1	Online shopping - Accessories, jewelry
2	Online shopping - Fashion, beauty
3	Online shopping - Sports and accessories
4	Online shopping - Health and fitness
5	Online shopping - Pet supplies
6	Air travel
7	Online courses and language resources
8	Online business, marketing, merchandising
9	Browser games - Online games
10	Hotels and vacations

use the persona categorization of Carrascosa et al. [6] for the top 50 personas, and resolve the taxonomy list[1] to obtain the related keywords. We group by the taxonomy keywords based on their content and then we form sets of labels describing the personas. For capturing active ad campaigns we use Google Search, as it reveals ad campaigns associated with products currently being advertised. That is, if a user searches for specific keywords (e.g., "men watches"), Google Search will provide a set of results, including a list of sponsored links from e-commerce sites and services conducting campaigns for the terms searched. This procedure is repeated until at least five, and a maximum of ten, unique domains per persona are collected from the Google Search results.

In general, our method is able to generate a large number of different personas, corresponding to various interests and online behaviors: from generic to specific taxonomy categories. As the effectiveness of a persona depends on the active ad campaigns at time, in our experiments we deploy only the 10 personas shown in Table 1.

Experimental Settings. Each experiment is executed multiple times (or runs), through parallel instantiations of the user devices within the implemented methodology. Each experimental run is executed following a timeline of phases as illustrated in Fig. 2. This timeline contains N sessions with three primary stages in each: Before, Mobile, and After. The *Before* (B_i) stage is when the two desktop devices perform a test browsing in parallel, before the mobile device is used, to establish the state of ads before the mobile device injects signal into the ad-ecosystem. The *Mobile* (M_i) stage is when the mobile device performs a train and a test browsing. This phase injects the signal from the mobile device during training with a persona, but also performs a subsequent test browsing with the control pages to establish the state of ads after the training. Finally, the

---

[1] https://www.google.com/basepages/producttype/taxonomy.en-US.txt.

After (A_i) stage is when the two desktop device perform the final test browsing to establish the state of ads after the mobile training.

After in-depth experimentation, we found that training time $t_{train} = 15\,\mathrm{min}$ and testing time $t_{test} = 20\,\mathrm{min}$ are enough for creating, collecting and processing a satisfying number of data without introducing noise to the web traffic, while keeping clear each device's signal to the ad-ecosystem. There is also a waiting time $(t_{wait} = 10\,\mathrm{min})$ and resting time $(t_{rest} = 5\,\mathrm{min})$ between the stages of each session, to allow alignment of instantiations of devices running in parallel during each session. In total, each session lasts 1.5 h and is repeated $N = 15$ times during a run.

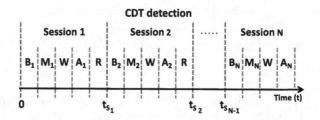

Fig. 2. Timeline of phases for CDT measurement. M_i: mobile training; $B_i(A_i)$: testing time before (after) mobile training; W(R): wait (rest) time.

Machine Learning Algorithms and Performance Metrics. Our analysis is based on three classification algorithms with different dependence on the data distribution. An easily applied classifier that can be used for performance comparison with the other models in a baseline fashion is Gaussian Naive Bayes. Logistic Regression is a well-behaved classification algorithm that can be trained as long as the classes are linearly separable. At last, Random Forest is a widely used learning method that constructs a multitude of decision trees at training time and outputs the class that is the mode of the classes of the individual trees.

A critical point when considering the performance evaluation of these algorithms is the selection of the appropriate metrics, since we want to report the most accurate estimation for the number of predicted paired devices, while at the same time measure the absolute number of misclassified samples overall. For this reason, metrics like Precision, Recall and F_1-score are typically used, since they can quantify this type of information. There is also one more metric used for measuring the dependence of the True Positive Rate (TPR) with the False Positive Rate (FPR). If we plot the curve of those two rates for different operational scenarios, we get the Receiver Operating Characteristic curve (ROC). If a single numeric score based on the ROC curve is needed, then the Area Under the Curve (AUC) is used.

3.2 Detecting CDT

This experimental setup emulates a realistic user behavior browsing frequently about some specific topics, but in short-lived sessions in her devices. Given that

Table 2. Performance evaluation for Random Forest. Left value in each column is the score for Class 0 (C0 = *not paired desktop*); right value for Class 1 (C1 = *paired desktop*).

Persona	Precision		Recall		F_1-Score		AUC
	C0	C1	C0	C1	C0	C1	
1	0.89	0.60	0.57	0.90	0.70	0.72	**0.73**
2	0.84	0.78	0.81	0.82	0.82	0.80	**0.82**
3	0.81	0.73	0.78	0.76	0.79	0.74	**0.76**
4	0.87	0.78	0.87	0.78	0.87	0.78	**0.82**
5	0.94	0.65	0.68	0.93	0.79	0.76	**0.80**
6	0.57	0.67	0.81	0.38	0.67	0.48	**0.59**
7	0.81	0.87	0.89	0.76	0.85	0.81	**0.81**
8	0.86	0.85	0.89	0.81	0.87	0.83	**0.84**
9	0.74	0.90	0.91	0.73	0.82	0.81	**0.81**
10	0.77	0.85	0.81	0.81	0.79	0.83	**0.81**

most users do not frequently delete their local browsing state, this setup assumes that the user's browser keeps all state, i.e., cookies, cache files, browsing history, etc. This assumption enables trackers to identify users easier across their devices, as they have historical information about these users. All 10 personas of Table 1 are used, while the data collection for each Persona lasts ∼4 days.

The classification results for the Random Forest algorithm, as reported in Table 2, had the best performance compared to the other two algorithms. We use AUC score as the main metric score, since the ad-industry seems to prefer higher Precision scores over Recall, as the False Positives have greater impact on the effect of ad-campaigns. As shown in Table 2, the model achieves high AUC score for most of the personas, with a maximum value of 0.84. Specifically, the personas 2, 4 and 8 scored highest in AUC, and also in Precision and Recall, whereas persona 6 has poor performance compared to the others.

In order to retrieve the variables that affect the discovery and measurement of cross-device tracking, we applied the feature importance method on the dataset of each persona, and selected the top-10 highest scoring features. Interestingly, features such as the day and time of the experiment, and the number of received ads are important for the algorithm to make the classification of the devices. Furthermore, time-related features are indeed expected to be important as they give hints on when the browsing signal was injected to the ad-ecosystem. In some cases, there were also landing pages that had high scoring, but this was not consistent across all personas.

These results indicate that for high scoring personas, we successfully captured the active CDT campaigns, but for the personas with lower scores, there may not be active cross-device tracking campaigns for the period of the experiments. Finally they also give credence to our initial decision to experiment in a continuous fashion with regular sessions injecting browsing signal, while at the same time measuring the output signal via the delivered ads.

4   Outcome and Future Directions

Undoubtedly, CDT has an impact on user privacy, but the actual extent of this tracking paradigm and its consequences to users, the community, and even to the ad-ecosystem itself, are still unknown. To this direction we proposed a concrete and scalable methodology that allows experimenting with different CDT scenarios. We plan to extend this work by designing and conducting various different experiments that will shed light and help understand the mechanics behind CDT as applied by the complex ad-ecosystem. Furthermore, the extensibility of the platform enables using new methods invented in the future for better input signal generation (e.g., for persona building), device emulation with more realistic browsing behavior, more precise webpage parsing for ads extraction, new machine learning algorithms etc. The proposed methodology will also enable the community of privacy researchers and advocates to study CDT in a systematic way, and to quantify its intensity and impact to users with different, and potentially sensitive or legally protected web interests and online behaviors.

Acknowledgments. This research has received funding from the European Union's Horizon 2020 research and innovation programme under Grand Agreement No. 700378 (project CIPSEC) and the Marie Sklodowska-Curie Grand Agreement No. 690972 (project PROTASIS). This paper reflects only the authors' view and the Agency is not responsible for any use that may be made of the information it contains.

References

1. FTC: Cross-device tracking. Technical report (2017)
2. Mavroudis, V., Hao, S., Fratantonio, Y., Maggi, F., Kruegel, C., Vigna, G.: On the privacy and security of the ultrasound ecosystem. Proc. Priv. Enhancing Technol. **2017**(2), 95–112 (2017)
3. Arp, D., Quiring, E., Wressnegger, C., Rieck, K.: Privacy threats through ultrasonic side channels on mobile devices. In: 2017 IEEE European Symposium on Security and Privacy (EuroS&P), pp. 35–47. IEEE (2017)
4. Brookman, J., Rouge, P., Alva, A., Yeung, C.: Cross-device tracking: measurement and disclosures. Proc. Priv. Enhancing Technol. **2017**(2), 134–149 (2017)
5. Zimmeck, S., Li, J.S., Kim, H., Bellovin, S.M., Jebara, T.: A privacy analysis of cross-device tracking. In: 26th USENIX Security Symposium, USENIX Security 2017, Vancouver, BC, pp. 1391–1408. USENIX Association (2017)
6. Carrascosa, J.M., Mikians, J., Cuevas, R., Erramilli, V., Laoutaris, N.: I always feel like somebody's watching me: measuring online behavioural advertising. In: Proceedings of the 11th ACM Conference on Emerging Networking Experiments and Technologies, CoNEXT 2015, pp. 13:1–13:13. ACM, New York (2015)

Incognitus: Privacy-Preserving User Interests in Online Social Networks

Alexandros Kornilakis$^{(\boxtimes)}$, Panagiotis Papadopoulos, and Evangelos Markatos

FORTH-ICS, Heraklion, Greece
{kornilak,panpap,markatos}@ics.forth.gr

Abstract. Online Social Networks have changed the way we reach news and information. An increasing number of people use social networks not only for communicating with friends and colleagues but also for their daily information needs. Apart from providing the users with personalized information in a timely manner, this functionality may also raise significant privacy concerns. The service provider is able to observe both the Pages a user is subscribed to and her inter- actions with them. The collected data can form a detailed user profile, which can later be used for several purposes; usually beyond the control of the user. To ad- dress these privacy concerns, we propose Incognitus: an approach to allow users browse Pages of OSNs without disclosing their interests or activity to the service provider. Our approach provides (i) a incognito mode of operation when browsing privacy-sensitive content. In this isolated, offline mode no tracking mechanisms can monitor the users behavior and no information can be leaked to the provider. At the same time, (ii) by using an obfuscation-based mechanism, Incognitus reduces the accuracy of the service provider when monitoring the interests of a user. Early results show that Incognitus has minimal bandwidth requirements and imposes reasonable latency to the users browsing experience.

1 Introduction

Online Social Networks such as Facebook, Twitter, Tumblr, Google+, Weibo, etc. do not constitute any more, a platform solely used by the users for communication and social interaction. The so-called model of "social broadcast" enables users, instead of searching and consuming news through traditional media or news websites, to have more personalized news delivered directly to them in a timely manner. According to a recent study [30], an increasing 67% of adults in the US get their news from social media; it was also found that social media now outperforms television as the major information source [34]. By providing a handy user interface OSNs enables users, through a publish-subscribe model, to subscribe/follow information providers who maintain *channels (or Pages)* and receive updates regarding the content they publish.

Of course, all this handy and timely superabundance of information does not come for free. In exchange for their monetarily free services OSN providers

© Springer Nature Switzerland AG 2019
A. P. Fournaris et al. (Eds.): IOSec 2018, LNCS 11398, pp. 81–95, 2019.
https://doi.org/10.1007/978-3-030-12085-6_8

deliver targeted advertisements to their users. To provide better-matched advertisements and suggestions a wide spectrum of user social interconnections [25], activity and interactions [22] has to be monitored. The OSN by monitoring the user's interactions with the content of such Pages - *links clicked, photos viewed, videos watched* - it is able to create a very detailed profile for every user containing information related to interests and preferences reconstructing thus parts of her actual personality [36]. While recently there is an increased awareness about privacy on social networks and a desire for data protection regularization [1], there are incidents [32] indicating that the user might have to take additional steps to protect her privacy.

In this paper, we are interested in protecting content considered as privacy-sensitive. For example, content related to politics, sexual orientation, religion or health issues. If a user follows a Page of a particular politician, the service may infer the user's political beliefs. We think that it is of the user's the main interest to protect such sensitive information. Thus the objective of this paper is to help users that although interested in receiving updates about privacy-sensitive issues, may not be willing to disclose their personal preferences and interests. Even if these users avoid subscribing to particular privacy-sensitive Pages thus choosing to manually fetch them every now and then, the service provider still can identify not only the fact that they requested for these Pages but also their interactions with the content.

The alternatives such a user has is to hide her actual identity: by creating a second disposable account to subscribe to the privacy-sensitive Pages she is interested in. Unfortunately, this approach would be subject to contamination since information from different web browsing sessions, such as browser or device fingerprints [2,7,24] or persistent and synced cookies [16,26] are able to correlate anonymous and eponymous browsing sessions revealing thus the true identity of the user [15,27]. To make matters worse, in popular online social networks disposable accounts is not an option [6] and having multiple fake accounts is not easy nowadays (some OSN's require a mobile phone number in order to register). To remedy this problem one might use a second account and a VM per browsing session over an anonymization network (such as Tor [12]) to hide the IP address aiming to finally limit cross-contamination. Of course the applicability of such approach (i.e. a combination of VM and Tor) in tablets and smartphones alongside the inconvenience it may cause to ordinary users, may repel most users. The user can always stop using OSNs to protect her privacy; however, there are a lot of organizations, associations, groups or communities that leverage the ease of message broadcasting and audience gathering in social networking platforms and do not maintain websites of their own outside the OSN. In this work, we propose a method to allow OSN users to protect their interests when anonymity is not feasible.

There are two distinct cases able to disclose a user's interests: (i) the actual fact that the user follows, likes or subscribes to a specific Page (ii) her interactions with this Page (navigating through past posts, watching videos or photos, etc.). In this paper, we propose *Incognitus*, a system to preserve the privacy of the users' interests against both cases. Our approach is twofold: we provide an obfuscation mechanism and an incognito mode of operation. In our system, the user follows/subscribes to an additional number of Pages which are used as noise. These additional Pages will reduce the accuracy of the service provider while trying to distinguish the noisy Pages from the real ones. After concealing the actual subscription our approach provides the user with a protected offline mode in which she can switch to whenever she wants access to a Page she considers as privacy-sensitive. In this isolated, offline mode of operation no requests or tracking mechanisms of the service provider can leak information about her activity and behavior.

To summarize, in this paper, we make the following contributions:

1. We propose a methodology to preserve the privacy of the sensitive interests of a user while browsing an OSN. Our approach provides an isolated protected mode of operation where no user monitoring can be applied by the curious service provider.
2. To assess the feasibility and effectiveness of our approach, we implemented our system as an extension for the Firefox browser using Facebook as our case study.
3. We experimentally evaluate our prototype and we show that it has minimal bandwidth requirements and adds reasonable latency to the user's browsing experience.

2   Motivation and Threat Model

In this paper, we assume the existence of an online social networking service, where there are several Pages maintained by organizations, authorities, corporations, groups or individuals (e.g. journalists, politicians, activists, doctors, etc.) to publish content and inform their audience about a particular subject. Such published content may include photos, articles, posts, links to external web pages, videos, etc. Users subscribe themselves to the Page in order to access this content and have updates delivered to their newsfeed in a timely manner.

Furthermore, we assume an honest online social networking service provider, which may try to identify the user's preferences in order to display personalized recommendations and advertisements matching the interests of the user. This service provider is capable of passively recording the user's activity at any time by observing her online interactions with a Page's content. This way, this provider knows: *When the user watches what video and for how long? When she browses what photo? On which photos she spends more time? What articles she reads?, What posts she reads and if she unfolds its related comments.* We assume that the service provider will not try to "cheat" by actively interfering with the process users are employing to protect their privacy, or try to gain more information than what a user is willing, or required, to give. We think that this assumption is valid since social networking service providers do not want to be hostile against their own users thus jeopardizing their reputation.

All this collected information about users' interests, is a property of the OSN and can be considered as an asset in case of future acquisition by another company [19,31]. In addition, this information could be later sold to advertisers [4,29] and used beyond the control of the user. We consider this tracking capability as a potential concern for the users' privacy and therefore in this paper, we aim to preserve the privacy of users who use OSNs to fulfill their daily information needs, users who use OSNs to get timely personalized news and not for communicating purposes. As a consequence, in this paper, we assume users that act as consumers of information, without being interested in posting, sharing or reacting [18] at any information related to the sensitive Page they are interested in. Such actions could allow a service provider by deploying term extraction and ML algorithms to identify the actual interests of the user.

3   Design Overview

The motivation behind our work is to build an offline incognito mode, to which the user can switch every time she feels like browsing a privacy-sensitive Facebook Page. In this isolated mode, no trackers would be able to monitor her behavior and interactions. In order for the user to browse this content, her browser needs to fetch the entire Page leaking this way to the service provider the fact that she is interested in navigating to this Page. As a consequence, the service provider can associate her interests with the related subject of the Page. To remedy this privacy infringement and reduce the accuracy of such association, we use an obfuscation-based approach, where we introduce noise, by encouraging the user to retrieve k more Pages used as noise.

3.1   Concealing the User's Subscriptions

Assume a user interested in a Page P, which deals with a privacy-sensitive issue: for example, the electoral campaign of a candidate. As soon as the user subscribes herself to this Page, the social network can consider with high probability that she is interested in the associated political party and hence infer her political preferences. In *Incognitus*, to reduce this certainty of the service provider when predicting the interests of its users, we encourage the user to subscribe, along with the Page P, to an additional number of $k-1$ Pages, which act as noise. By obfuscating this way her choices, the service provider will get subscribe requests for k Pages without being able to accurately identify the Page she is actually interested in.

Parameter k practically defines the amount of noise introduced in the user's profile. By fine tuning this obfuscation number, users are able to achieve the level of privacy they are comfortable with. Very small values of k may increase the confidence of a service provider and disclosure the actual interests of the user. On the other hand, very high values of k may skyrocket the overhead and the bytes downloaded in her browser, since *Incognitus* will download more noise Pages and content.

Selection of Noise

All such noise Pages are randomly chosen from a publicly accessible list SP of "privacy-sensitive" Pages, which is shared among all users. In *Incognitus*, these $k - 1$ noise Pages are chosen randomly with uniform probability from SP. As a consequence, when a user subscribes to k Pages (i.e. P+noise) the probability for the service provider to identify the one the user is actually interested in, is $1/n$. Note at this point that apart from the P, the $k - 1$ noise Pages are not fake and also privacy-sensitive. It is apparent, that users enable *Incognitus* to specifically conceal Pages that consider sensitive, the use of non sensitive Pages as noise would help the service provider easily filter out those Pages. By using the same SP list for all users, *Incognitus* allows for every Page a user may use as noise, to appear some other users that are indeed interested in it and hence subscribed to it.

Of course, not all Pages enjoy the same popularity. In case of a user interested in a very popular Page (e.g. 30% of the total users are already subscribed to it), a service provider may pinpoint the very popular Page among the $k - 1$ others and assume that most probably this Page is the one the user is interested in. To mitigate such cases, instead of uniform selection of noise Pages, one can use a proportional selection, already proposed in related studies [28], based on the size of the Pages' audience. This would lead to a selection of noise Pages with similar popularity to the Page the user is actually interested in.

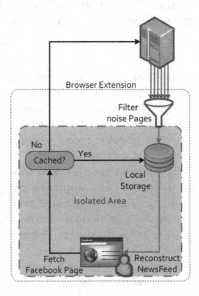

Fig. 1. High level overview of Incognitus. Incognitus provides the same browsing experience, while the user is able to browse the privacy-sensitive content incognito.

3.2 Concealing the User's Interactions

Apart from the subscriptions of a user to Pages, her interests can be also leaked by monitoring her behavior, while browsing a Page. Specifically, even after obfuscating her subscriptions, the service provider may track her interactions (e.g. clicks, mouse hovers etc.) and distinguish which Pages she fetches to use as noise and which Pages she fetches because she is actually interested in.

To remedy this leak, *Incognitus* stores the entire content of a privacy-sensitive Page locally (e.g. posts, videos, photos, etc. along with their metadata) and whenever the user browses this Page, it intercepts the HTTP requests to the web server and instead retrieves the content from the disk. As a consequence, an isolated offline mode is created allowing the user to interact with the content (e.g. view a photo) without allowing the service provider to learn about it. To achieve the same user experience, *Incognitus* reconstructs the user's NewsFeed by transcoding on-the-fly incoming components. This way, in case of privacy-sensitive content (e.g. posts) originated from privacy-sensitive Pages the links to the associated components will point to the local stored files.

Of course, whenever *Incognitus* downloads the content of a Page P to store it locally, and in order for the content request of Page P to remain obfuscated, it also downloads the content of the rest $k - 1$ Pages as well (although it does not need to store it). This way, the service provider will see a bunch of identical HTTP requests for content, being unable to identify the noise requests. Such *update* operation of *Incognitus* is performed asynchronously in the background, so it cannot degrade the user's browsing experience by imposing additional latency.

The Delta Approach

Its easy to anticipate that downloading bulk content from multiple pages, every time a user browses Page P, may put an unbearable load to the browsing experience, causing a significant increase not only to the rendering latency but also to the required bandwidth. To avoid such overhead, *Incognitus*, on the background and periodically, downloads any possible recent updates of Page P and stores them locally. This way, whenever a user needs to fetch P, the browser extension will use the pre-fetched content from the disk and thus render the content in zero time. In addition, by using the delta approach *Incognitus* downloads less bytes from the network, avoiding re-fetching content every time the user browses P. Note again that like above *Incognitus* does not download only the deltas of Page P but the deltas of all k privacy-sensitive Pages the user has subscribed to.

In summary, we can see in Fig. 1 a high level overview of the internal design of *Incognitus*. It periodically (i) retrieves the deltas from all k Pages, (ii) filters them to discard the noise (i.e. posts from noise Pages) providing the exact same browsing experience as before and (iii) stores locally the content of P (i.e. html, images, photos, videos, json files etc.). When the user opens her NewsFeed, the served html gets transcoded and the links of the components, originated from P, are rewritten to point to the local stored content.

4   Sensitive Pages

In this section, we describe how the list SP of sensitive Pages is formed in *Incognitus*. We first present the web-based indexing service, responsible for distributing the list SP. Then we describe how this list gets its elements updated and how the users, by sending anonymous requests, can add Pages they consider sensitive to the next version of this list. Finally, we discuss how the Page indexing service may control the size of SP to keep it smaller than a desired threshold and what *Incognitus* does in case of disappearing sensitive Pages.

5   A Web-Based Indexing Service

To be effective, our system needs to make sure that all of its users share the exact same list SP of sensitive Pages. The rationale behind it is that users' random selections of "noise" Pages from SP, contribute to hide the Pages other users are interested in, which belong to SP, too. Therefore, upon installation, but also periodically, *Incognitus* downloads the final version of this list from a publicly accessible web index.

We envision that this web index along with the list SP and the project in general would be maintained by the broader community of users. Such privacy-concerned communities already support similar volunteer-based projects, such as Tor [5]. The list SP can be seeded by an initial set of sensitive Pages and further improved through human intervention and participation of the community.

5.1   Updating the List of Sensitive Pages

Initially, SP can contain a set of commonly used sensitive Pages from several different categories. Nevertheless, new sensitive Pages may arise, or users may want to subscribe to a sensitive Page that is not included in SP. Thus, there is a need to update the list of sensitive Pages dynamically based on the users needs. To accommodate this necessity, we propose a publicly accessible web-based indexing service that hosts the latest version of the list SP with the sensitive Pages. *Incognitus*, which runs transparently at the client-side as a browser extension, periodically communicates with this service to receive the updated list of sensitive Pages. This way, each user is equipped with the latest version of SP, which includes any newly added sensitive Page.

Apart from that, the indexing service must be able to accept user requests for new Pages to be included in SP. These requests must be performed, through *Incognitus* transparently and anonymously. To achieve this, whenever a user wants to subscribe herself to a sensitive Page, *Incognitus* intercepts the "subscribe" request and checks whether this Page already exists in SP. If so, *Incognitus* subscribes the user to the noise selection described in Sect. 3. If the Page does not exist in SP, the user can ask *Incognitus* to consider this Page as sensitive from now on and thus include it in the next version of SP. After that,

Incognitus communicates anonymously with the indexing service counterpart, sending a request with the new Page to be added.

It is important that this communication, between the user and the indexing service to be anonymous without revealing either the identity or the IP address of the user. Hence, the user would need to trust no indexing service, and consequently the indexing service would not ever learn which user asked for what Page to be added. To achieve such anonymous communication, *Incognitus* uses a network anonymizer (i.e. Tor [5]) when sending requests for the sensitive Page index.

In addition, to avoid any timing correlations, *Incognitus*, upon sending a request to include a new Page in SP, waits for a reasonable period of time before actually subscribing the user to this Page (and noise Pages). This way, it ensures that there will be a number of other users that will have downloaded the updated version of SP, which includes the newly added Page.

5.2   Controlling the Size of Sensitive Page List

Eventually, the new additions of sensitive Pages will end up increasing significantly the size of the list. As a result, each sensitive Page in SP will have less probability to get selected as noise in case of uniform noise selection. This, as a consequence, would decrease the efficiency of *Incognitus* since for a Page P a user is interested in, there must be a number of other users using it as noise, in order for the service provider not to be able to distinguish who uses it as noise and who does not. To address this issue, the indexing service is responsible to keep SP in the desirable size. Specifically, when SP exceeds a predefined size threshold, it automatically removes from SP the less important Pages, i.e., less popular Pages, less active Pages, or the older ones based on the date they were inserted in SP. This way, the most important Pages, which are more popular, active, or were recently added to SP, will remain in the list of sensitive Pages. Note that if a user wants to subscribe to a Page that has been previously removed from SP, she can re-insert it any time through the procedure we describe above.

5.3   Disappearing Pages

While using *Incognitus*, $k - 1$ noise channels are selected and used as noise for every sensitive Page a user is actually interested in and subscribes to. These batch of noise Pages remain constant over time. However, it is theoretically possible that some of the Pages included in this batch k will disappear at some point in time. Indeed, people may choose to delete their accounts, corporations may go out of business, or organizations may change their focus. In such cases, their Page (say D) in the online social network will be deleted or it will become inactive. This will create two kinds of problems:

First, people who used to be subscribed to D cannot just stop being subscribed to it. Moreover, they cannot stop being subscribed to the noise Pages, which were selected along with D, too. If the users unsubscribe from the above Pages, the service provider will immediately correlate D's disappearance with the users' change of subscribing patterns, and figure out that the users were actually interested in Page D. Fortunately, this not particularly worrisome. Indeed, the users should continue being subscribed to D along with their selected noise Pages. They will just pay a small overhead in downloading content from Pages they do not need anymore.

The second problem is that people who included D among their noise Pages may be more exposed to the service provider. Indeed, if their noise Pages start disappearing one after the other, it seems that the service provider will be in a better position to find what is the Page they are really interested in. An obvious approach would be to add other noise Pages in the place of the disappeared ones. Unfortunately, this is not correct, as the service provider will easily figure out that both the disappeared ones as well as the recently subscribed ones are noise Pages. Surprisingly, the best approach for the users is to *do nothing*: they should just keep being subscribed to the Pages even if they disappear one after another all the way to the last one. The key observation here is that both users who are interested in D as well as users who are not interested in D but have just included D as noise, should do the same thing: *nothing*. In this way, the service provider will not be able to differentiate, which users are interested in D and which are not.

6 Implementation

In order to evaluate the feasibility and efficiency of *Incognitus*, we have implemented an extension for the popular browser of Mozilla Firefox. As a case study, we used the online social network of Facebook. In this social network, we assume users interested in subscribing to Facebook Pages.

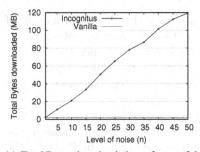
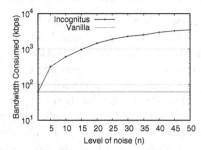

(a) Total Bytes downloaded as a factor of the different level of noise

(b) Average bandwidth consumption as a factor of the different level of noise

Fig. 2. The overhead of noise in terms of additional downloaded bytes, when a user browses a sensitive Page for the first time with no previously stored content

Facebook Pages [9] are for businesses, brands and organizations to share content and can be customized by publishing stories, hosting events, adding apps and more. A user who subscribe to a Page can get timely updates directly delivered in her account's NewsFeed. On Facebook, a NewsFeed is a list of updates on user's Facebook home page. NewsFeed includes status updates, photos, videos, links, app activity and Likes from people, Pages and groups that the user is subscribed to on Facebook.

In *Incognitus* browser extension, the user can subscribe to a sensitive Page, by using the standard Facebook Like button (either from inside the Facebook platform or from a website by using the appropriate Facebook widget). To achieve the same user experience, in *Incognitus* we intercept all Like requests and check whether they correspond to a Page considered as sensitive (i.e. if the corresponding Page is included in the SP). If so, the extension based on the k parameter set by the user, on the background, randomly selects the additional $k - 1$ Pages from the list SP of sensitive Pages, which will be used as noise. Finally it sends a Like request to each one of the k (real and noise) sensitive Pages. The browser extension, internally, keeps the list of the noise Pages it has used and the real Page with which they are associated (Fig. 2).

Our prototype implementation is built using the Firefox Add-on SDK [23], due to the convenience it provides regarding the access of the browser extensions to the local storage. In addition, it is developed using Javascript along with JQuery and Mutation Summary libraries [35] according to the Facebook documentation [11] and policies [10].

7   Performance Evaluation

For *Incognitus*'s performance evaluation, we used a PC equipped with an AMD FX-6300 processor (3.5 GHz, 8 MB L3 Cache) and 8 GB RAM. We populated the set S with 60 Pages of categories we personally consider as privacy-sensitive: medical diseases, political parties, sexual preferences, etc.

Bandwidth Consumption: It is easy to anticipate that the introduction of noise leads to an increased bandwidth consumption in order to obfuscate the sensitive transmitted information. The traffic volume that is generated depends on the noise level the user has chosen; specifically, on the value of parameter k. This parameter practically denotes that, with our system, the user roughly downloads k times more bytes.

First, we monitor the traffic generated from the user's browser when visiting a sensitive Page, for several values of k. In this experiment, we measure the consumed bandwidth in the worst case: when the user visits the Page for the first time and there is no pre-stored content on her disk. At Fig. 3, we observe the total bytes downloaded and at Fig. 4 the traffic load generated, for different levels of noise, both for a user subscribed to a sensitive Page. Moreover, we include the vanilla case $k = 1$, when *Incognitus* is disabled. We noticed that the bandwidth consumed is reasonably low compared to the vanilla case, adding less than an order of magnitude overhead in case of $k = 10$.

It is worth recalling at this point, that these results regard the first fetch of a Page where no data are stored on disk. After the first fetch, the delta approach

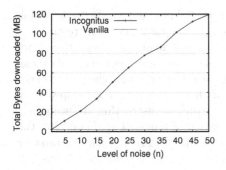

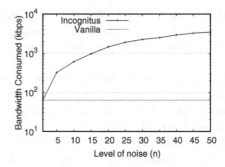

Fig. 3. Total bytes downloaded as a factor of the different level of noise

Fig. 4. Average bandwidth consumption as a factor of the different level of noise

is used as we describe at Sect. 3. Then, *Incognitus* periodically downloads the updates from all sensitive Pages, both noise, and real ones. This way, we are able to reduce both the latency imposed and the bandwidth consumed, since we retrieve the content from the disk instead of fetching data from the Facebook server. In the following experiment we measure (i) the total bytes downloaded when the user browses P without having any content pre-fetched on disk and (ii) the average bytes downloaded periodically with the delta approach.

To quantify the bandwidth consumption over time, we perform measurements with our prototype for 30 min. Specifically, we subscribe to a sensitive Page and fetch it for the first time, without having any content previously stored on the disk. In Fig. 5, we plot the results of this experiment using 3 different values of k, the vanilla case ($k = 1$), a low one ($k = 5$), and a higher one ($k = 25$). As we see, there is an increased spike at the beginning, when the browser downloads the content for the first time, after that the bandwidth consumed is close to zero. In this figure, we also see the periodic delta mechanism at 10th and 20th-minute where *Incognitus* checks for updates.

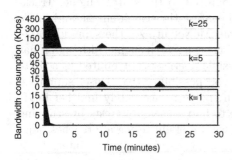

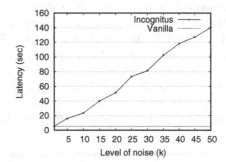

Fig. 5. Bandwidth consumed as a factor of time for the initial fetch and the delta updating mechanism.

Fig. 6. Average rendering latency as a function of different level of noise, the first time a user browses a sensitive Page.

Browsing Latency: The most important aspect that can degrade the browsing experience of a user is latency: the time needed to render and show to the user the content she is waiting for. In the following experiment, we set out to explore the delay imposed by *Incognitus* when the user visits a privacy-sensitive Page. In this experiment we inspect the worst case scenario: when the user fetches the Page as soon as she subscribes to it and therefore no data were previously locally stored. In this scenario, *Incognitus* before reconstructing the web-page the user requested to see, has to download the set of k noise Pages and filter the noise content. As a consequence, we fetch a sensitive Page P with our browser extension enabled and we measure the time it takes to load the Page's full content. We run the experiment 100 times for different noise levels and in Fig. 6 we plot the results. As expected, the higher the amount of noise we add, the larger the imposed latency is. We see that for $k = 10$ the additional latency is about 22 s, which we believe is unable to harm the users browsing experience; at the same time, the privacy of her interests is preserved. We have to note that, this latency does not correspond to an optimal scenario. The actual Page is always at the last position in the sensitive set, while at the same time, the background fetch of sensitive pages is performed sequentially; thus, latency could be further reduced by leveraging the multiprocess architecture and the HTML5 Web Workers API of modern browsers.

8   Related Work

Our work's foundations lie in the concept of k-anonymity [33]. K-anonymity provide privacy guarantees that the individuals who are the subjects of a released dataset cannot be re-identified. With K-anonymity an individual cannot be distinguished from at least k-1 individuals whose information also appear in the data. L-diversity [21] and [20] extend k-anonymity by handling some of the weaknesses.

TrackMeNot [13] is a Firefox add-on designed to achieve privacy in web search by obfuscating user's queries within a stream of programmatically-generated decoys. For each real query submitted to the search engine, Track-MeNot also submits additional queries to confuse the search engine and introduce doubt for the user's real queries. TrackMeNot utilizes the same idea (i.e. obfuscation) to protect user's privacy when using a search engine, although it has one fundamental difference: the set of possible queries is not limited to a finite set as Facebook Pages do. So there is a good possibility that a user submits a rare query, which would enable the search engine to accurately find her interests. Moreover, an adversary may be able to find a user's interests by studying successive sequences of queries [3] and make use of clustering approaches [8].

In [28] authors propose k-subscription to conceal the user's interests in microblogging services. Their approach relies on introducing noise in order to decrease the disclosure probability of the service provider. They propose and evaluate two algorithms to compute the necessary amount of noise that needs to be used based on the popularity of the channel the user is interested in following.

Although k-subscription is related to our work, it assumes that users subscribe to a channel using the standard mechanism (e.g., follow) that the microblogging service offers. In *Incognitus*, we assume users that may avoid subscriptions thus browsing content from Pages manually and we assume service providers that deploy more aggressive behavioral tracking techniques, monitoring any action the user may perform with a Page's content.

Single sign-on (SSO) services (like Facebook Login [14]) often improve the user's browsing experience by offering a convenient way to register to third party websites and adding a social dimension to the user's experience. But their existence and popularity also raise significant privacy concerns, since third-party Web sites are granted access to personal information. In addition, the social network can observe the Web sites that the user visits as well. To mitigate that problem, SudoWeb [17] proposes a system that enables users to surf the Web using downgraded sessions with the single sign-on platform, i.e., stripped from excessive or personal information, and with a limited set of privileged actions. Although both SudoWeb and *Incognitus* belong to the domain of privacy-preserving browsing, SudoWeb focus on enhancing the user's privacy when visiting third-party Web sites and not when browsing an OSN.

9   Conclusion

Online social networks have changed the way we fulfill our daily information needs. However, using OSN's for information consumption is a double-edged sword. The low cost and timely access to information come with a cost to user's privacy: the online social network provider is able to collect information regarding its users' interests, which sometimes may regard privacy-sensitive topics.

To cope with this situation, we propose *Incognitus*: a tool to (i) allow users to browse Pages with privacy-sensitive content in an offline mode, without disclosing their interactions to the service provider. And at the same time, (ii) by using an obfuscation-based mechanism conceal the privacy-sensitive topics a user is interested in, thus reducing the accuracy with which the service provider can determine the user's interests. We implemented our approach as a browser extension using Facebook as a case study. Our experimental evaluation shows that *Incognitus* has minimal bandwidth requirements and imposes reasonable latency for a normal amount of noise, when at the same time is able to adequately preserve the privacy of the actual interests of the user.

Acknowledgement. The research leading to these results has received funding from European Unions Marie Sklodowska-Curie grant agreement No 690972. The paper reflects only the authors view and the Agency and the Commission are not responsible for any use that may be made of the information it contains.

References

1. What does the general data protection regulation (GDPR) govern? March 2016. https://ec.europa.eu/info/law/law-topic/data-protection/reform/what-does-general-data-protection-regulation-gdpr-govern_en
2. Acar, G., Eubank, C., Englehardt, S., Juarez, M., Narayanan, A., Diaz, C.: The web never forgets: persistent tracking mechanisms in the wild. In: Proceedings of the 2014 ACM SIGSAC Conference on CCS (2014)
3. Balsa, E., Troncoso, C., Diaz, C.: OB-PWS: Obfuscation-based private web search. In: IEEE Symposium on S&P 2012 (2012)
4. Brown, M.S.: When and where to buy consumer data (and 12 companies who sell it) (2015). http://www.forbes.com/sites/metabrown/2015/09/30/when-and-where-to-buy-consumer-data-and-12-companies-who-sell-it
5. Dingledine, R., Mathewson, N., Syverson, P.: Tor: the second-generation onion router. In: Proceedings of the 13th Conference on USENIX Security Symposium, SSYM 2004, Berkeley, CA, USA, vol. 13, pp. 21. USENIX Association (2004)
6. Drake, N.: Help, I'm trapped in Facebook's absurd pseudonym purgatory (2015). http://www.wired.com/2015/06/facebook-real-name-policy-problems
7. Eckersley, P.: How unique is your web browser? In: Atallah, M.J., Hopper, N.J. (eds.) PETS 2010. LNCS, vol. 6205, pp. 1–18. Springer, Heidelberg (2010). https://doi.org/10.1007/978-3-642-14527-8_1
8. Elovici, Y., Shapira, B., Meshiach, A.: Cluster-analysis attack against a private web solution (PRAW). Online Inf. Rev. **30**(6), 624–643 (2006)
9. Facebook business. Facebook pages (2017). https://www.facebook.com/business/products/pages
10. Facebook for developers. Facebook platform policy (2016). https://developers.facebook.com/policy/
11. Facebook for developers. Facebook developer documentation (2017). https://developers.facebook.com/docs/
12. Greenberg, A.: Why Facebook just launched its own "dark web" site (2014). https://www.wired.com/2014/10/facebook-tor-dark-site/
13. Howe, D.C., Nissenbaum, H.: TrackMeNot: resisting surveillance in web search. In: Lessons from the Identity Trail: Anonymity, Privacy, and Identity in a Networked Society, vol. 23, pp. 417–436 (2009)
14. Facebook Inc.: Facebook login (2018). https://developers.facebook.com/docs/facebook-login/
15. Johansson, F., Kaati, L., Shrestha, A.: Timeprints for identifying social media users with multiple aliases. Secur. Inf. **4**(1), 1 (2015)
16. Kamkar, S.: Evercookie - virtually irrevocable persistent cookies (2010). http://samy.pl/evercookie/
17. Kontaxis, G., Polychronakis, M., Markatos, E.P.: Minimizing information disclosure to third parties in social login platforms. Int. J. Inf. Secur. **11**(5), 321–332 (2012)
18. Krug, S.: Reactions now available globally (2016). https://newsroom.fb.com/news/2016/02/reactions-now-available-globally/
19. Kumar, M.: Why Facebook is buying Whatsapp for $19 billion? (2014). http://thehackernews.com/2014/02/why-facebook-is-buying-whatsapp-for-19.html
20. Li, N., Li, T., Venkatasubramanian, S.: t-closeness: privacy beyond k-anonymity and l-diversity. In: 2007 IEEE 23rd International Conference on Data Engineering, pp. 106–115. IEEE (2007)

21. Machanavajjhala, A., Kifer, D., Gehrke, J., Venkitasubramaniam, M.: l-diversity: privacy beyond k-anonymity. ACM Trans. Knowl. Discov. Data (TKDD) **1**(1), 3 (2007)
22. Mander, J.: Why Facebook is tracking time spent on newsfeeds (2015). http://www.globalwebindex.net/blog/why-facebook-is-tracking-time-spent-on-newsfeeds
23. Mozilla developer network and individual contributors. Add-on SDK (2016). https://developer.mozilla.org/en-US/Add-ons/SDK
24. Papadopoulos, E.P., Diamantaris, M., Papadopoulos, P., Petsas, T., Ioannidis, S., Markatos, E.P.: The long-standing privacy debate: mobile websites vs mobile apps. In: Proceedings of the 26th International Conference on World Wide Web, WWW 2017, Republic and Canton of Geneva, Switzerland, pp. 153–162. International World Wide Web Conferences Steering Committee (2017)
25. Papadopoulos, P., Chariton, A.A., Athanasopoulos, E., Markatos, E.P.: Where's Wally? How to privately discover your friends on the internet. In: Proceedings of the ASIACCS 2018 (2018)
26. Papadopoulos, P., Kourtellis, N., Markatos, E.P.: Cookie synchronization: everything you always wanted to know but were afraid to ask. arXiv preprint arXiv:1805.10505 (2018)
27. Papadopoulos, P., Kourtellis, N., Markatos, E.P.: Exclusive: how the (synced) cookie monster breached my encrypted VPN session. In: Proceedings of the 11th European Workshop on Systems Security, EuroSec 2018 (2018)
28. Papadopoulos, P., Papadogiannakis, A., Polychronakis, M., Zarras, A., Holz, T., Markatos, E.P.: K-subscription: privacy-preserving microblogging browsing through obfuscation. In: Proceedings of the ACSAC 2013 (2013)
29. RT. Privacy betrayed: Twitter sells multi-billion tweet archive (2012). https://www.rt.com/news/twitter-sells-tweet-archive-529/
30. Shearer, E., Gottfried, J.: News use across social media platforms (2017). http://www.journalism.org/2017/09/07/news-use-across-social-media-platforms-2017/
31. Singer, N., Merrill, J.B.: When a company is put up for sale, in many cases, your personal data is, too (2015). http://www.nytimes.com/2015/06/29/technology/when-a-company-goes-up-for-sale-in-many-cases-so-does-your-personal-data.html
32. Solon, O.: Facebook says Cambridge Analytica may have gained 37m more users' data (2018). https://www.theguardian.com/technology/2018/apr/04/facebook-cambridge-analytica-user-data-latest-more-than-thought
33. Sweeney, L.: k-anonymity: a model for protecting privacy. Int. J. Uncertainty Fuzziness Knowl. Based Syst. **10**(05), 557–570 (2002)
34. Wakefield, J.: Social media 'outstrips TV' as news source for young people, June 2016. https://www.bbc.com/news/uk-36528256
35. Weinstein, R.: Mutation summary (2015). https://github.com/rafaelw/mutation-summary
36. Youyou, W., Kosinski, M., Stillwell, D.: Computer-based personality judgments are more accurate than those made by humans. Proc. Nat. Acad. Sci. **112**(4), 1036–1040 (2015)

Vulnerability and Malware Detection

Deep Ahead-of-Threat Virtual Patching

Fady Copty[✉], Andre Kassis, Sharon Keidar-Barner, and Dov Murik

IBM Research, Haifa, Israel
fadyc@il.ibm.com

Abstract. Many applications have security vulnerabilities that can be exploited. It is practically impossible to find all of them due to the NP-complete nature of the testing problem. Security solutions provide defenses against these attacks through continuous application testing, fast-patching of vulnerabilities, automatic deployment of patches, and virtual patching detection techniques deployed in network and endpoint security tools. These techniques are limited by the need to find vulnerabilities before the 'black hats'. We propose an innovative technique to virtually patch vulnerabilities before they are found. We leverage testing techniques for supervised-learning data generation, and show how artificial intelligence techniques can use this data to create predictive deep neural-network models that read an application's input and predict in real time whether it is a potential malicious input. We set up an ahead-of-threat experiment in which we generated data on old versions of an application, and then evaluated the predictive model accuracy on vulnerabilities found years later. Our experiments show ahead-of-threat detection on LibXML2 and LibTIFF vulnerabilities with 91.3% and 93.7% accuracy, respectively. We expect to continue work on this field of research and provide ahead-of-threat virtual patching for more libraries. Success in this research can change the current state of endless racing after application vulnerabilities and put the defenders one step ahead of the attackers.

Keywords: Virtual patching · Application vulnerability · Deep learning

1 Introduction

Every application has bugs and vulnerabilities. Some of them can be exploited by hackers, also known as 'black hats,' to gain control over the software, get credential information, or leak data. Both hackers and software developers invest a lot of effort in discovering these bugs. Hackers look for the next loophole, while developers try to detect and fix vulnerabilities before they are exploited. When hackers detect the vulnerability or when the application is not properly updated before the vulnerability is made public, we witness catastrophes such as the WannaCry campaign or Heartbleed bug.

Software verification and penetration testing are the usual means to detect these vulnerabilities. As software becomes more complex, verification has become an almost impossible challenge. Software testing methods cannot cover all possible scenarios, even with highly effective heuristics such as fuzz testing using genetic algorithms [2]. Software verification methods based on formal verification can cover all corner cases; however, they cannot scale to verify industrial-scale software.

© Springer Nature Switzerland AG 2019
A. P. Fournaris et al. (Eds.): IOSec 2018, LNCS 11398, pp. 99–109, 2019.
https://doi.org/10.1007/978-3-030-12085-6_9

How do hackers succeed despite the software testing applied? The "bad guys" have an advantage: once a vulnerable software is deployed it is not always patched immediately, even once a vulnerability is detected. This occurs because it takes time to design and implement a fix that will not affect the application's performance and user experience. The vulnerability may be in legacy code, which is hard to maintain, or the software may have been written by a third-party organization. Often the patch is simply delayed. According to Infosecurity Magazine [7], companies take an average of 100 to 120 days to patch vulnerabilities.

In the most difficult cases, the software cannot be patched because it is highly critical and cannot suffer from instability that may be associated with the fix. One example of this would be flight control software. Moreover, the software may be installed on a device that cannot be easily patched, such as a pacemaker.

The Internet of Things (IoT) is even harder to protect. When a patch is released, it must be deployed on many endpoints. Moreover, the many sensors and devices have an endless variation of software that needs to be installed, managed, and protected.

Solutions for virtual patches are introduced in cases where the software is not patched. Instead of patching the software, a virtual patch blocks malicious inputs that may exploit the vulnerabilities in the software. The virtual patch can be deployed as part of the firewall, or in the case of IoT, as part of the gateway. In network firewalls and proxies, such as ModSecurity and Snort, virtual patches are manually written rules that protect the software [13, 18]. There is a configurable layer to which rules can be added. This capability makes the virtual patching process much easier than the traditional patching process, especially for cases in which the software cannot be patched at all. The main disadvantages of this method are that it requires human effort and can be applied only for known vulnerabilities.

Since software will never be free of bugs, mitigation systems such as Intrusion Detection Systems (IDS) [12] were developed to detect malicious software-input in real time. There are two types of IDS: misuse and anomaly detection systems. Misuse systems are based on signatures to avoid time consuming content inspection. For each malicious software-input, a signature is created and added to a black list. Any software-input with a signature on the blacklist is blocked. The problem is that IDS are not effective against variations of the malicious software-input; these can be easily created by making minor changes to the software-input or using different testing techniques. The effectiveness of an IDS is highly dependent on its ability to update signatures, which requires human effort. Anomaly-based IDS learns what constitutes normal behavior for the system and alerts when it detects a deviation from the normal behavior. Unfortunately, some types of attack appear as normal behavior. Both IDS methods have a low probability of detecting zero-day attacks. In addition, IDS suffer from a high rate of false positive and false negatives, which may lead them to block legitimate software or grant access to malicious software.

We introduce a novel, fully-automated, approach that provides ahead-of-threat virtual patching for security loopholes. This approach leverages fuzz testing technology, based on genetic algorithms, to create data for a machine learning algorithm. The algorithm then learns which inputs need to be blocked. No human effort is required to analyze the software vulnerabilities, no effort is required to label the training data, and prior knowledge on the vulnerabilities in the software is not mandatory. The virtual patch is a deep neural network (DNN) predictive model. It can be produced by an application developer from source code and used as an application hardening method. It can also be produced by a security vendor from source code or binary and deployed in a deep inspection IDS or endpoint protection tool for file scanning.

2 Related Work

The fields of virtual patching and intrusion detection are heavily researched, both in the industry and in academia. Mishra et al. [12] provide an extensive survey of intrusion detection techniques applied to many levels in a cloud environment. According to their categorization, our approach is classified as a misuse detection technique with a decision engine trained by machine learning. This is as opposed to signature-based misuse detection, which is prone to overlooking novel attack patterns.

Many recent IDS implementations use machine learning techniques. Kim et al. [8] use SVM to build a machine-learning based IDS. Li et al. [9] propose an artificial neural network (ANN) based IDS. Pandeeswari et al. [14] employ a hybrid algorithm of Fuzzy C-Means clustering and ANN. Ashfaq et al. [3] use a semi-supervised learning approach to intrusion detection to reduce the number of labeled examples needed to train the model. Aljawarneh et al. [1] use anomaly detection and a hybrid approach of seven different ML algorithms to improve accuracy and maintain a low false positive rate. These authors base their decision on network traffic metadata. In contrast, our solution is trained on the actual data content (packet payload, file content) and can detect malformed, potentially malicious, packets and files. It can be used in addition to an IDS deployed at the network level or at the host level.

Our ability to detect malicious payloads using deep neural networks resembles work in the field of static malware detection using deep learning [16, 17]. However, most of these works rely on the availability of a large training set of benign and malicious samples, which are used to train the machine learning model. Our solution generates its own training set from a small corpus of examples and monitors the target application's execution on each sample input to decide that input's label.

3 Overview

Our solution takes an application's source code or binary, and automatically produces an ahead-of-threat virtual patch of the application. The virtual patch predicts–in real time—whether an input to an application will allow a vulnerability to be exploited in this application. The system can be divided into two components: (1) data set generation using testing techniques and (2) supervised learning using deep neural networks. The data set generation is described in Sect. 3.1, and the supervised learning is described in Sects. 3.2 and 3.3. Sections 3.4 and 3.5 describe the training and evaluation methods.

3.1 Data Set Generation Using Testing Techniques

Using deep learning techniques necessitates a large data set with diverse samples. Our work requires a large corpus of relevant inputs to the application that we are trying to protect. The corpus should include benign samples that the application can process, error samples that the application recognizes and rejects, and malicious samples that expose an application vulnerability. To build such a corpus, we used the software testing technique of fuzzing, which is usually used to find bugs or security vulnerabilities. We use a side effect of fuzzing: the millions of inputs that are generated during the fuzzing process. As part of our solution, we have the 'fuzzer' label these inputs as benign, error, or malicious, thereby forming a training set we can use to build our model.

Our data set generation effort relies on AFL [2] to generate the test cases and to exercise the application (running it with the generated inputs). We use AFL along with an address sanitizer to detect malicious tests. A test is labeled malicious if AFL shows that it crashes the application, or if it fails one of the sanitizer checkers. We made two modifications in AFL to support our requirements: we save non-unique test cases and save error cases as their own class. These modifications are described in detail below.

Saving Non-unique Test Cases. AFL saves only unique input files; therefore, input files that hit an execution path that was already covered by other inputs are not added. While this is beneficial for creating a minimal corpus that covers the application's execution paths, we want to save many different inputs for each path to train our model. We added an option for AFL to save non-unique inputs.

Saving Error Cases. AFL categorizes inputs into two classes: benign and crash. Crashes cause abnormal program termination, often via an OS signal that indicates some memory access error. We added an option to detect error files by either recording the program exit code (where a non-zero exit code means the input is detected as an error) or by detecting output to the standard error stream (where output in standard error means the input is detected as invalid).

3.2 Automatic Feature Extraction

Typical IDS systems must operate in a real-time environment. This is the reason we selected feature-extraction methods that limit the inspection time to milliseconds, from the moment the file is received until a decision is made.

We deploy two techniques for feature extraction; counting the number of occurrences of a specific token in a file, and transforming the file byte sequence into a one-dimensional numerical vector and applying zero-padding. We explored the use of token bi-gram, but experiments showed that this exceeded our time limitations.

To create the token count features, we first determined what tokens to count. These tokens can be divided into two groups. The first group of tokens are any dictionary tokens received as optional input from the user. This group covers most of the expected input-language tokens. However, security vulnerabilities are often caused by strings not in this token group.

The second group of tokens is generated automatically using the genetic algorithm. A genetic test generation algorithm performs either a mutation or a crossover [19] on a chosen test to create a new test. We captured all successful mutations and used them as tokens. This type of token often corresponds to tokens that were not specified in the input-language specification, but were implemented in the application under test. This can happen due to poor specification or poor implementation.

3.3 Deep Learning

The structure of the deep neural network as depicted in Fig. 1 is composed of two paths. These paths eventually combine into one output that predicts the probability of malicious versus benign. We used Keras Deep Learning Models with Scikit-Learn in Python [4, 15] to implement this structure. The total number of parameters in our DNN model is around five million.

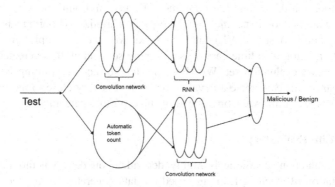

Fig. 1. Structure of deep neural network

In the first path of our deep neural network, we apply zero padding and transform every test into a numerical one-dimensional vector of a constant size. We feed this vector into a convolutional neural network (CNN) and later into a recurrent neural network (RNN). The CNN in this path is responsible for detecting input-language tokens and patterns, while the RNN is responsible for detecting the sequential order of those patterns. The CNN is composed of eight layers; a combination of one-dimensional convolution, LeakyReLu, and MaxPooling layers. The RNN is a bi-directional Long-Short-Term-Memory (LSTM). This path is highly scalable and requires no prior feature extraction. We achieved good performance using only this path; however, adding the second path provided us with a boost in accuracy performance.

In the second path, count-features are extracted from an input test and fed into a convolution neural network. The sequential order of these count-features is naturally arbitrary; therefore, there is no need for memory elements in the deep neural network (DNN) of this path and a feed forward network is sufficient. We use a convolution neural network to capture any combination of features that might be important for our classification. The CNN in this path is composed of nine layers of a combination of one-dimensional convolution, LeakyReLU, Dense, and MaxPooling Layers. Eventually, both paths are combined using a Softmax layer.

3.4   Training and Evaluating Performance of the DNN

We used the testing techniques to generate millions of samples of the data, which were then classified as benign, malicious, or error. We merged the error and malicious classes. This is a safe practice, since the final results of predicting an error sample as malicious and blocking it, or running it on the application and yielding an error, are essentially the same.

To imitate a real-life situation where vulnerabilities are not yet discovered and evaluate our ahead-of-threat predictions, we split the data into training set and evaluation (testing) set by setting up a time barrier. The time barrier was set such that 99% of the unique test paths fall into the training set, and only 1% fall into the evaluation set. This is an imitation of the real-life continuous testing environment, in which various parties test an application in parallel and the only synchronization point is the Common Vulnerability and Exposure (CVE) database. Next, we used all samples created by the data generation before this time barrier as a training set, and all those created after this time barrier as an evaluation set. We chose not to use random splitting into test and evaluation, since this can create an evaluation set that is very close to the training set, which is not effective in evaluating ahead-of-threat virtual patching.

3.5   Real Life Evaluation

The above evaluation technique is highly dependent on data generation. This is a known limitation of machine learning based on data generation techniques. To overcome this and to evaluate on real life data, we trained the DNN on an old version of the application and used publicly available CVE examples produced years after the release of this version. We then imitated an attacker technique of fuzzing the CVE to get many permutations of the same CVE. We used those permutations to evaluate our ahead-of-threat capability.

To make sure that the ahead-of-threat capability stems up from the predictive DNN and not from the testing algorithm, we executed all the data generated on a new version of the application-under-test and verified they do not expose vulnerability on it.

4   Experimental Results

To evaluate the system we held the ahead-of-threat patching experiments on two open-source libraries and attempted ahead-of-threat patching on six CVEs. We conducted the experiments on LibXML2 [11] and LibTIFF [10]. Table 1 shows the version of the library we used for data generation and the version we used for real-life evaluation.

Table 1. Libraries used in the experiment

Tested library	Version for data generation	Version for evaluation
LibTIFF	3.71	4.0.7
LibXML2	2.6.32	2.9.3

4.1 Data Generation

To generate LibXML2 tests we ran AFL on the LibXML2 parser utility testReader from LibXML2 v2.6.32. This testing utility parses input XML files. We ran AFL along with an address sanitizer for three days to generate and classify XML files into three categories: benign, error, and malicious. We used the library's test-corpus as an initial test corpus for AFL and provided XML tokens as a dictionary for AFL. AFL created several millions of non-unique xml files, and the genetic algorithm discovered approximately 200 new tokens. The number of error tests generated far outnumbered the tests in other classes. We merged the error and malicious classes into one class and applied random under-sampling on the error/malicious class. We then calculated the time barrier such that the ratio between unique malicious samples in the training set compared to the evaluation set would be 99 to 1%. This process provided us with approximately 600,000 train samples and about 150,000 evaluation samples, where benign and error/malicious classes are equal in the number of samples.

We performed the same process for LibTIFF 3.71 and used the tiffdump utility found in the LibTIFF library. This process provided us with about 300,000 train samples and around 1,100,000 evaluation samples. The large bias towards evaluation samples can be explained by the fact that it is very hard to find new unique tests in later stages of the fuzz testing. Thus, the 99 to 1% cut of the unique tests forces an early time barrier on the data generation, while most non-unique tests are found in the later stages.

We limited the size of the numerical vector fed into the first DNN path to 500 and configured the DNN training to run for 4 epochs. We then trained our DNN on the LibXML2 data set using the automatically extracted features and received the following results on the evaluation set. Table 2 shows the confusion matrix of this evaluation. This yields an accuracy of 89.7% and F1 score of 89.6%.

Table 2. Confusion matrix for LibXML2

	Predicted benign	Predicted malicious/error
True benign	70,400	3,400
True malicious/error	11,818	61,982

We performed the same training on the LibTIFF data, and it produced the results shown in Table 3. This yields an accuracy of 86.6% and F1 score of 86.6%. In Fig. 2 we show the receiver operator characteristic (ROC) curves for both models, giving an area under curve (AUC) of 95% for LibXML2 and 98% for LibTIFF.

Table 3. Confusion matrix for LibTIFF

	Predicted benign	Predicted malicious/error
True benign	523,762	11,228
True malicious/error	129,424	405,566

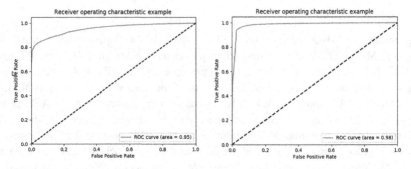

Fig. 2. ROC curve for LibXML2 (left, AUC = 95%) and LibTIFF (right, AUC = 98%)

4.2 Real-Life Evaluation

We downloaded LibXML2 and LibTIFF exploit proof-of-concept (PoC) files from the publicly available Exploit Database [5]. Table 4 shows the CVE PoC that we downloaded, date of disclosure, last vulnerable version, release date of the library used for data generation, and the ahead-of-threat years calculated by the difference between the disclosure date and the release date of the library version used for data generation.

Table 4. List of vulnerabilities tested with ahead-of-threat patching

Library	CVE ID	Disclosure date	Last vulnerable version	Release of the library used for data generation	Ahead-of-threat in years
LibXML2	CVE-2015-8806	2015-05-08	2.9.3	April 2008	7
	CVE-2016-1833	2015-11-24	2.9.3		7
	CVE-2016-1838	2016-02-24	2.9.3		8
LibTIFF	CVE-2017-9147	2017-05-12	4.0.7	Dec 2004	13
	CVE-2017-9936	2017-06-26	4.0.8		13
	CVE-2017-10688	2017-06-29	4.0.8		13

We started by validating that the tests we generated in our data-generation phase do not expose any vulnerability in the last vulnerable version of each library. This validated that we are truly generating an ahead-of-threat patching, and not merely an automatic virtual-patch.

Next, we downloaded benign XML and TIFF files from Wikipedia's database XML source code and the FileFormat database [6], respectively. We started to create a test set for the real-life examples by fuzzing the latest vulnerable version of each library using AFL, and the downloaded benign and the CVE PoC files as initial test corpus. This ensured that samples in the malicious class are new tests to our DNN, never found before during the data generation phase, and that the benign and error classes were created from a previously unseen test corpus.

We ran AFL on libXML2 using these initial test corpuses and created tests to get $\sim 20,000$ benign tests, $\sim 33,000$ error, and $\sim 107,000$ malicious tests. Next, we merged the error and malicious classes and under sampled them to get $\sim 20,000$ tests. We ran AFL on LibTIFF and got $\sim 10,000$ benign, 0 error, and $\sim 18,000$ malicious. Since our main attention is on the malicious, we ignored the empty error class and under sampled the malicious to get $\sim 10,000$ error/malicious class.

Next, we tested all those samples on the predictive DNN that we trained earlier and received the following results. Table 5 shows the confusion matrix for LibXML2 results, showing an accuracy of 91.3% and F1 score of 91.3%. Table 6 shows the confusion matrix for LibTIFF results, showing accuracy of 93.7% and F1 score of 94.3%. In Fig. 3 we show the ROC curves with AUC of 83% for LibXML2 and 96% for LibTIFF. We see that the ROC for LibTiff looks rather smooth, while the ROC for LibXML2 shows a drastic jump around False Positive Rate $\cong 17\%$. We attribute this to the difficulty in creating a good real-life evaluation set for a library starting from a small number of CVE examples.

Table 5. Real-life evaluation confusion matrix for LibXML2

	Predicted benign	Predicted malicious/error
True benign	15,622	3,192
True malicious/error	1	18,297

Table 6. Real-life evaluation confusion matrix for LibTIFF

	Predicted benign	Predicted malicious/error
True benign	105,550	6,498
True malicious/error	9,308	131,729

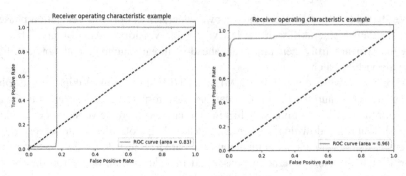

Fig. 3. Real life evaluation ROC curve for LibXML2 (left, AUC = 83%) and LibTIFF (right, AUC = 96%)

5 Discussion, Conclusion, and Future Work

We demonstrated how our approach can be used to automatically analyze an application and generate a virtual ahead-of-threat patch. The effort required to test, debug, and fix an application is often very expensive in late stages of the application life cycle. This prevents developers from performing thorough root cause analysis of the application vulnerability. Therefore, they end up adding some error condition that blocks the path to the vulnerability rather than to the vulnerability family. We argue that or approach performs better than the human developer in root cause analysis and in generalizing the benign and error/malicious examples it views to patch a wide family of vulnerabilities. Thus, it does a better job of predicting ahead-of-threat vulnerabilities.

Our next challenge is to apply this approach to virtually patch IoT devices. The need for virtual patches in IoT is even higher in critical devices such as pacemakers. Furthermore, we will study the effect of deploying a virtual patch on a gateway that may block inputs before communicating with the device, compared to deploying a virtual patch on the device itself. Another research direction is expanding the possible targets for patching: our experiments show the effectiveness of this method for C/C++ code; we plan to develop fuzzing techniques for JavaScript programs that will build a system to virtually patch cloud services. Fuzzing of dynamic languages introduces new challenges, such as understanding the underlying memory model. However, we believe it is essential to make our approach applicable to modern software as well.

Acknowledgements. This project has received funding from the European Union's Horizon 2020 research and innovation programme under grant agreement No. 740787 (SMESEC). We would like to thank Ayman Jarrous and Tamer Salman for fruitful discussions, and Ben Liderman for help in building the automated framework.

References

1. Aljawarneh, S., Aldwairi, M., Yassein, M.B.: Anomaly-based intrusion detection system through feature selection analysis and building hybrid efficient model. J. Comput. Sci. **25**, 152–160 (2018). https://doi.org/10.1016/j.jocs.2017.03.006
2. American Fuzzy Lop (AFL) Fuzzer. http://lcamtuf.coredump.cx/afl/. Accessed 22 July 2018
3. Ashfaq, R.A.R., Wang, X.Z., Huang, J.Z., Abbas, H., He, Y.L.: Fuzziness based semi-supervised learning approach for intrusion detection system. Inf. Sci. **378**, 484–497 (2017). https://doi.org/10.1016/j.ins.2016.04.019
4. Chollet, F.: Keras (2015). https://keras.io. Accessed 13 Aug 2018
5. Exploit Database. https://www.exploit-db.com/. Accessed 22 July 2018
6. FileFormat.info TIFF samples. http://www.fileformat.info/format/tiff/sample/. Accessed 22 July 2018
7. Infosecurity Magazine. https://www.infosecurity-magazine.com/news/companies-average-120-days-patch/. Accessed 22 July 2018
8. Kim, G., Lee, S., Kim, S.: A novel hybrid intrusion detection method integrating anomaly detection with misuse detection. Expert Syst. Appl. **41**(4), 1690–1700 (2014). https://doi.org/10.1016/j.eswa.2013.08.066
9. Li, Z., Sun, W., Wang, L.: A neural network based distributed intrusion detection system on cloud platform. In: Proceedings of the 2nd International Conference on Cloud Computing and Intelligent Systems (CCIS), pp. 75–79. IEEE Press, New York (2012). https://doi.org/10.1109/ccis.2012.6664371
10. LibTIFF. http://www.simplesystems.org/libtiff/. Accessed 22 July 2018
11. LibXML2. http://xmlsoft.org/. Accessed 22 July 2018
12. Mishra, P., Pilli, E.S., Varadharajan, V., Tupakula, U.: Intrusion detection techniques in cloud environment: a survey. J. Netw. Comput. Appl. **77**, 18–47 (2017). https://doi.org/10.1016/j.jnca.2016.10.015
13. ModSecurity virtual patching. https://www.linkedin.com/pulse/fix-without-touching-virtual-patching-web-modsecurity-rafael-pinto/. Accessed 22 July 2018
14. Pandeeswari, N., Kumar, G.: Anomaly detection system in cloud environment using fuzzy clustering based ANN. Mob. Netw. Appl. **21**(3), 494–505 (2016). https://doi.org/10.1007/s11036-015-0644-x
15. Pedregosa, F., et al.: Scikit-learn: machine learning in python. JMLR **12**, 2825–2830 (2011)
16. Raff, E., Barker, J., Sylvester, J., Brandon, R., Catanzaro, B., Nicholas, C.: Malware detection by eating a whole exe. arXiv preprint (2017)
17. Saxe, J., Berlin, K.: Deep neural network based malware detection using two dimensional binary program features. In: Proceedings of the 10th International Conference on Malicious and Unwanted Software (MALWARE), pp. 11–20. IEEE Press, New York (2015). https://doi.org/10.1109/malware.2015.7413680
18. Snort Network Intrusion Detection & Prevention System. https://www.snort.org/. Accessed 23 July 2018
19. Srivastava, P.R., Kim, T.H.: Application of genetic algorithm in software testing. Int. J. Softw. Eng. Appl. **3**(4), 87–96 (2009)

Malware Clustering Based on Called API During Runtime

Gergő János Széles[1,2(✉)] and Adrian Coleşa[1(✉)]

[1] Computer Science Department, Technical University of Cluj-Napoca,
Cluj-Napoca, Romania
adrian.colesa@cs.utcluj.ro
[2] Cyber Threat Proactive Defense Lab, Bitdefender, Cluj-Napoca, Romania
jszeles@bitdefender.com

Abstract. Malware growth was exponential in the last years, therefore it is a tedious work to manually analyze them in order to observe when a new strain appears. In this article we present a dynamic analysis system which clusters suspicious executable files in different malware families, based on the behavioral similarities their running processes exhibit thus reducing the workload of malware analysts. We identified similarities between our approach and the problem of text clustering based on topic, achieving similar results to text clustering without semantic analysis involved. We modeled the behavior of a process by extracting sequences of Windows API functions called by that process during its execution. We separated the registered API calls on three levels, based on their impact on the system, and dealt with them as text-like terms. More complex terms were constructed with N-grams and the features were represented with TF-IDF scores. We clustered the processes with variants of the *k-means* algorithm and derived a method for analyzing cluster characteristics in order to determine the best number of clusters to be considered. Finally, we identified the API level and N-gram lengths required to obtain relevant clusters.

Keywords: Behavioral analysis · k-means · Windows API

1 Introduction

The apparition of ransomware and cryptocurrency mining malware [15], along with the increasingly advanced and sophisticated obfuscation techniques such as packing and polymorphism resulted in a great increase in the number of observed malicious files in recent years. In 2018, by the end of the second quarter the quantity of malware already exceeded last year's threshold [2]. AV-TEST reported a number of 350000 new hashes observed daily. In the wild this number is even bigger, as there are lots of malware samples which are not observed in the wild, or are not collected in their honeypots.

Considering these aspects, security researchers are overwhelmed by the amount of malware files (samples) they need to manually analyze and may fail

© Springer Nature Switzerland AG 2019
A. P. Fournaris et al. (Eds.): IOSec 2018, LNCS 11398, pp. 110–121, 2019.
https://doi.org/10.1007/978-3-030-12085-6_10

to observe when a new strain of malware appears. This increases the need of automating the process of dynamic analysis and clustering files whose processes manifest similar behavior. The results of grouping files can then be used to identify if a sample is part of an already known family or a new one, and also allows malware analysts to select only relevant samples from groups for detailed manual analysis.

When it comes to extracting behavioral information from processes there are two fundamental strategies to choose from. Static analysis [4] tries to extract a sequence of function calls from the binary of the file without running it. While this approach has a reduced execution time, it can be easily evaded if a malware is packed/encrypted or it resolves its called functions at run-time [9]. Dynamic analysis consists of running a sample in a controlled environment [25] and monitoring it's behavior. Behavioral information can be extracted from the Windows API functions the process calls, from the system resources it modifies (file system, registry), network traffic etc. Some solutions for malware clustering are proposed in [17, 19], however these solutions consider independent API calls as features. We observed that sequences of function calls generally describe an action better, therefore we have used N-grams of function names as features. Another method proposed in [3] tracks operating system objects and operations upon them, thus describing behavior with sequences of functions which operate on the same resources which describe some malware better, however it omits some functions which do not operate directly on system resources, therefore eliminating extra behavioral information.

Our research consists of modeling the registered behavior of malicious processes by text files containing sequences of API calls, clustering the malware samples by their behavioral similarity and evaluating which model yields the most relevant data in order to perform good clustering.

We achieved this by first grouping Windows API calls on different levels by their impact upon the system. We intercepted the functions called by an analyzed process and registered their names in the order they were called in a text file. This way such a text file describes a process' behavior, where called function names are equivalent to words in a text. Therefore behavior-based process clustering is equivalent to text clustering. We used *tf-idf* score [13, 18, 22] to determine the importance of each term (i.e. N-grams constructed from function names) in the whole document corpus (i.e. set of analyzed malware). Then we applied variants of the *k-means* algorithm to cluster the malware samples in families and analyzed the formed clusters and to determine the accuracy of our labeling. We could then draw some conclusions about how the levels of API calls and the length (i.e. the value of N) of N-grams influenced the results of our clustering and observed similarities between text clustering and malware clustering methods.

The main contribution of our paper are:

- define possible behavior models with different levels of detail provided by the Winows API calls;
- provide a method to determine number of possible clusters on the dataset, as well as clustering the samples from that set.

The paper' structure is the following: Sect. 2 presents a general overview of our system, Sect. 2.1 describes how API calls are grouped on different levels of detail, Sect. 3 describes the way our behavioral model was transformed into a text-like model, Sect. 4 presents the clustering algorithms used, Sect. 5 interprets the results obtained while Sect. 6 compares our results to other existing solutions, finally in Sect. 7 we present the conclusions drawn and possible further improvements.

2   System Overview

The system that we developed takes as input a set of recent malware files (samples) that still perform their malicious actions. We aim to form clusters of suspicious/malicious executable files such that those which manifest similar behavior get grouped together. In order to do this we run each of them individually in a virtual machine, monitoring and registering the behavior of their processes by sequences of function calls from the Windows API. Although these sequences can be extracted statically from the binary file [24], this method has its limitations in constructing the execution flow of a process, therefore we chose to dynamically analyze the samples to obtain a temporal ordering of the function calls. An overview of the system we developed is shown in Fig. 1.

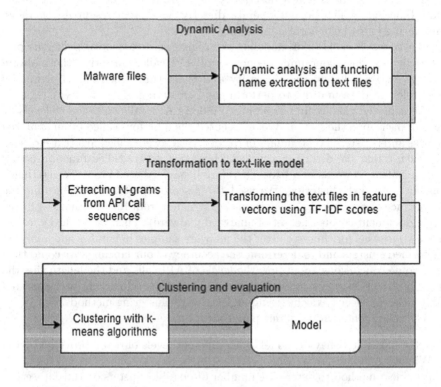

Fig. 1. Overview of our malware analysis and clustering framework

2.1   Recorded Windows API Functions

We grouped the function calls from the Windows API we recorded on three levels. We considered both the severity of the changes a function can bring over the system and how close a function is to the kernel. This way we distinguished the following three levels:

1. *api_level_1*: is the lowest one, containing most of the system calls from *ntdll.dll* which modify any state of the registry, create processes, alter memory contents or perform file system operations. Example functions include NtCreateKey, NtSetValueKey, NtCreateProcess, NtWriteFile, NtAlpcConnectPort, etc.;
2. *api_level_2*: in addition to *api_level_1* it contains functions from *kernel32.dll* and *user32.dll*, which could be higher level versions of system calls, or perform operations which do not have big impact on the system (e.g., mutex creation, module loading, etc.) Example functions: RegCreateKey, CreateProcessW, WriteFile, LoadLibrary, etc.;
3. *api_level_3*: is the highest and richest one, containing all of the functions from *level_1 and level_2* and other API calls, which have no direct interaction with the operating system's kernel and have no impact on the system, but could bring extra information for the malware analyst (e.g. clipboard operations, modifying keyboard layout for different languages, etc.).

The analysis system runs the samples in a controlled environment (e.g. a virtual machine). The system of sandboxes we used was based on QEMU virtual machines, due to the fact that it is not the most popular virtualization engine, therefore there are very few malware which can identify that they are being run in a sandbox. The virtual machines also contain anti-evasion techniques (e.g., changed process names of some monitoring tools, protecting modules of our function extractor, etc.). Our system then generates the trace of API function names ordered by the timestamp of their call and saves them to log files that will be extracted from the sandbox. This is done with the help of a minifilter driver which ensures that for each newly created process the module which logs the called functions is loaded into its address space. The driver also provides an extra layer of security, given by the fact that it runs in kernel-mode while the malware will run in user-mode, on a higher level. This way we can ensure the integrity of our monitoring tool and of the log files it generates. In Fig. 2 we can see the structure of an API dump file. In the first part it contains a header which offers information about the sample which was run (i.e. process name, hash, etc.) and about the environment (i.e. executable path, timestamp, etc.). The header is being followed by the sequence of API calls which offer information about the function name, the API level, the timestamp of the call, the parameters, etc. The API level was used to create three datasets. Each set contained behavioral information about the same malware samples, but it was represented by filtering the functions from the corresponding level.

```
{
  "Type":"ApiDump",
  "ProcessName":"Te1b7cd639e0ac906d267298769230bc.exe",
  "Pid":2764,
  "ParentPid":"2968",
  "ParentPath":"\\Device\\HarddiskVolume2\\tools\\timelog.exe",
  "StartTime":"0x01D348326CFF43DF",
  "NStartTime":"0x0000002C70EBBA1B",
  "OsStartTime":"0x01D348326CFF43DF",
  "NParentStartTime":"0x0000000000000000",
  "OsParentStartTime":"0x0000000000000000",
  "ExecutablePath":"\\Device\\HarddiskVolume2\\ux\\Te1b7cd639e0ac906d267298769230bc.exe",
  "CommandLine":"c:\\ux\\Te1b7cd639e0ac906d267298769230bc.exe",
  "ParentCommandLine":"C:\\tools\\timelog.exe c:\\ux\\Te1b7cd639e0ac906d267298769230bc.exe 360 C:\\share\\ping
  "MD5":"0xEE187CD639E0AC906D267298769230BC",
  "Api":[
    {
      "Func":"ZwOpenKey",
      "ApiLevel":2,
      "Depth":0,
      "Timestamp":200711580131,
      "Dll":"ntdll.dll",
      "Tid":"2760",
      "FuncId":1,
      "ApiOrder":1,
      "RetAddr":"0x779C87B8",
      "IsCorrupted":false,
      "Params":[
        {
          "Name":"KeyHandle",
          "Type":"PHANDLE",
          "Value":"0x0"
        },
        {
          "Name":"DesiredAccess",
          "Type":"DWORD",
          "Value":"0x3"
        },
        {
          "Name":"ObjectAttributes",
          "Type":"POBJECT_ATTRIBUTES",
          "Value":" 0x840084, (null)"
        }
      ],
      "Return":{
        "Type":"UINT32",
        "Value":"0xC0000034"
      }
    },
```

Fig. 2. API dump file header and first function from sequence

3   The Text-Like Model

We took the files generated at the previous step and saved only the function names in a list, each name representing a word. Then we extracted N-grams of words, varying N from 1 to 9. The purpose of considering longer N-grams was to try to group sequences of function calls into meaningful behavioral characteristics. For example in the case of the classic code injection the sequence *VirtualAlloc* → *VirtualProtectEx* → *WriteProcessMemory* → *CreateRemoteThread* describes the complete malicious action, while a single *VirtualAlloc* call simply allocates memory and it is a legitimate action. For each value of N we created different text files where the terms were the N-grams. Our goal was to find the value of N for which the best clustering could be achieved. In Fig. 3 the construction of terms in text files is shown for different values of N. The original list of APIs in this example would be *ZwOpenKey, ZwSetInformationProcess, ZwQueryAttributesFile, ZwCreateSection, ZwProtectVirtualMemory, LoadLibraryExW, ZwAlpcConnectPort, ZwAlpcSendWaitReceivePort*

The next step was to transform our text files into feature vectors, in order to be able to apply clustering algorithms on them. One way to achieve the transformation is to compute the *tf-idf* score [22] for each term in our text files. The *tf* acronym stands for "term frequency" and represents the number of times a word (i.e. term) appears in a document. We normalized this value by dividing it by the length of the document. The *idf* acronym stands for "inverse document frequency" and represents the total number of documents in the corpus divided

```
N = 1                          N = 3
ZwOpenKey                      ZwOpenKey-ZwSetInformationProcess-ZwQueryAttributesFile
ZwSetInformationProcess        ZwSetInformationProcess-ZwQueryAttributesFile-ZwCreateSection
ZwQueryAttributesFile          ZwQueryAttributesFile-ZwCreateSection-ZwProtectVirtualMemory
ZwCreateSection                ZwCreateSection-ZwProtectVirtualMemory-LoadLibraryExW
ZwProtectVirtualMemory         ZwProtectVirtualMemory-LoadLibraryExW-ZwAlpcConnectPort
LoadLibraryExW                 LoadLibraryExW-ZwAlpcConnectPort-ZwAlpcSendWaitReceivePort
ZwAlpcConnectPort
ZwAlpcSendWaitReceivePort
```

Fig. 3. Text file with N-grams for N = 1 and N = 3

by the number of documents in which a specific term appears. This means that terms which describe a topic (i.e. in our case, sequences of functions that describe a behavior) better, will get a higher score, while a term which appears in every document will be considered irrelevant. The *tf-idf* score is therefore computed as it is described by (1).

$$tf\_idf(term, doc) = \frac{freq(term, doc)}{\sum_{t' \in d} freq(t', doc)} \cdot log\left(\frac{|corpus|}{|\{d \in corpus : term \in d\}|}\right) \quad (1)$$

This way each sample will be described as an m-dimensional vector where each N-gram is a term and its coefficient is its *tf-idf* score.

4 Clustering Strategy

We used variants of k-means with *kmeans++* seeding [1] for clustering our samples. The algorithm is highly dependent on the initial centroids chosen randomly, therefore we ran each case 50 times and chose the best convergence. We used k-means initially and then we switched to mini-batch k-means [23] for better scaling, as the latter algorithm converges faster when the number of samples is large. We performed cluster analysis on the resulting models to determine the number of clusters which form naturally on the dataset. The next step was to evaluate if our clustering was accurate by comparing the predicted labels with the ground truth. We observed that spherical k-means [5] performs better, due to the fact that it projects points onto the unit sphere and therefore uses cosine distances for vectors unlike traditional k-means which uses Euclidean distance.

We analyzed each model with the help of internal metrics [10] in order to determine the number of clusters that can be formed on the dataset. These metrics do not take into account any ground truth, they only describe the quality of clusters. We aimed to have good *compactness* (i.e. distances inside a cluster to be as small as possible) and *high separation* (i.e. distances between clusters to be as big as possible).

The first metric we used was the mean value of the *Silhouette score (S)* [21] for each sample, described in Eq. (2), where a is the mean distance between the sample and other points inside the cluster and b is the mean distance between the sample and all the points in the nearest cluster. A value close to 1 indicates well-separated clusters, while a value close to 0 means overlapping clusters.

$$S = \frac{b - a}{max(a, b)} \tag{2}$$

The second metric was the *Calinski-Harabasz score (CH)* [6], which reflects both compactness and separation at the same time and its value should be as high as possible. We could compute it by calculating the ratio of the *between-cluster dispersion* and the *within-cluster dispersion*, as described in Eq. (3).

$$CH(k) = \frac{Tr(B_k)}{Tr(W_k)} \cdot \frac{N - k}{k - 1} \tag{3}$$

The third metric we used was the *Davies-Bouldin (DB) index* [8], which is described in Eq. (4) and uses *intra-cluster variance* and *inter-cluster center distance* to find the worst pair of clusters (which are close and scattered), therefore our goal was to find the minimal value.

$$DB = \frac{1}{NC} \sum_i max_{j \neq i} \frac{\frac{1}{n_i} \sum_{x \in C_i} d(x, c_i) + \frac{1}{n_j} \sum_{x \in C_j} d(x, c_j)}{d(c_i, c_j)} \tag{4}$$

5   Evaluation

In order to test our system, we collected 40 000 trending malicious samples from our honeypots and submissions from the real-world. Then we took 4 200 files about which we knew that they were distributed evenly between 5 clusters, each of them representing a malware family (*Emotet, GrandCrab, Cerber, PWS/Hacktool, ClipBanker*) and each group contains behaviorally similar samples.

We first evaluated the number of clusters our classification system formed on these samples by running k-means on each set, varying the number of clusters (i.e. k) from 2 to 100. However for large cluster numbers (≥ 20) the internal metric scores, described below, tended to stabilize at extreme values. This is expected behavior due to the fact that if we divide our dataset in more clusters, they will contain fewer elements and they will be grouped based on specific actions they perform, not by the malware family they represent. Therefore we only considered cluster numbers from 2 to 15.

We correlated the three internal metrics described above by plotting them for each cluster number k and choosing the maximum possible value for Silhouettes and Calinski-Harabasz, while taking the minimum value of the Davies-Bouldin index. In Fig. 4 the absolute value for each score is displayed. We can determine from these values that the ideal cluster number in this case is 5, because the Davies-Bouldin index abruptly gets to a local minimum from point 4 to point 5 and it remains around that value, the Calinski-Harabasz score is decreasing, therefore a smaller value for k favors this score and the Silhouettes score is growing, therefore earlier values, like 3 or 4 are not suitable. However when these values are not so well distinguished, in order to eliminate confusion we can plot the values on a normalized scale, in order to see their changes in value,

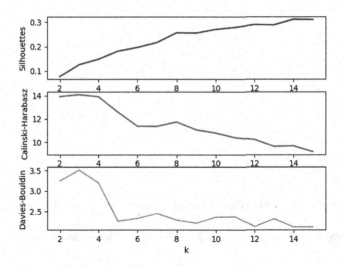

Fig. 4. Evaluation of the clustering process. In this example the optimal number of clusters is 5

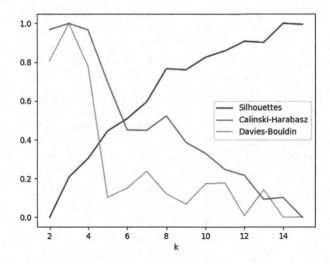

Fig. 5. Normalized values for internal metrics. When the changes are observed relative to each other, the cluster number can be more easily determined

relative to each other. The same example set is used in Fig. 5 and the value for k can be more obviously determined, if we correlate the three internal metrics.

We also evaluated the *accuracy* of the model obtained from the best value for k with the help of *V-measure* [20] and *purity*, which is simply the number of correctly labeled samples divided by the total number of samples. Then we ran spherical k-means for the same k to determine the accuracy of our clustering. The results are shown in Table 1.

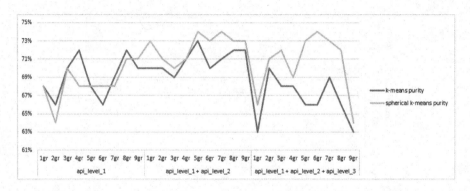

Fig. 6. Purity scores for standard k-means and spherical k-means

Table 1. Resulting values for different API levels and N-grams

	N-grams	Optimal k	V-measure	Purity	Spherical purity
api_level_1	1gr	6	0.27	68%	68.5%
	2gr	4	0.33	66%	64%
	3gr	5	0.37	70%	70%
	4gr	6	0.39	72%	68%
	5gr	7	0.34	68%	68%
	6gr	5	0.33	66%	68%
	7gr	4	0.37	69%	68%
	8gr	6	0.38	72%	71%
	9gr	6	0.42	70%	71%
api_level_1 + api_level_2	1gr	6	0.33	70%	73%
	2gr	5	0.35	70%	71%
	3gr	5	0.32	69%	70%
	4gr	6	0.34	71%	71%
	5gr	5	0.40	73%	74%
	6gr	5	0.37	70%	73%
	7gr	5	0.36	71%	74%
	8gr	5	0.40	72%	73%
	9gr	5	0.45	72%	73%
api_level_1 + api_level_2 + api_level_3	1gr	4	0.20	63%	66%
	2gr	6	0.30	70%	71%
	3gr	6	0.30	68%	72%
	4gr	6	0.28	68%	69%
	5gr	6	0.25	66%	73%
	6gr	5	0.24	66%	74%
	7gr	6	0.28	69%	73%
	8gr	6	0.27	66%	72%
	9gr	4	0.22	63%	64%

For better visualization we plotted the purity of the standard k-means clustering and the same score for spherical k-means. As we can see in Fig. 6 the best results can be observed for the sample sets containing `api_level_2` calls. Generally the best clustering can be done if we create N-grams of 5 and 7 terms, due to the fact that if fewer calls are taken into account, we might lose behavioral semantic, while too many calls result in increased noise. When choosing `api_level_3` calls, the noise becomes too high for good clustering and for accurate results. However the spherical k-means algorithm still handled this situation well.

6 Related Work

In [3] a novel dynamic analysis system is proposed which extracts behavioral profiles for samples by constructing relations between API calls and then using those behavioral characteristics as features. They obtained impressive results, however the data set was labeled automatically by taking only samples which were detected uniformly by several AV vendors, which led to a set which contained easy to cluster samples [14, 16]. Our solution took evenly distributed clusters and the files were labeled by behavioral similarity instead of AV detection names.

Some simpler models were proposed in [17, 19] where the function parameters were taken into account in order to obtain details about behavior. However these solutions consider API calls along with arguments as individual features, while an approach similar to text clustering, by using N-grams leads to more consistent results.

In text clustering field there are many solutions based on N-grams and *tf-idf* models [7, 12] which are very efficient, but they all pre-process the text with various semantic analysis methods. These methods could be applicable to some extent in the behavioral modeling field and it could be researched further. However when we compare our solution with text clustering without semantic analysis [11] we can observe that our results are similar or in some cases even better than those of the text clustering problem.

7 Conclusions

In this paper we presented our research on trying to find a suitable behavioral model for malware samples such that files of the processes which share similar behavior can be clustered together. We identified similarities with text clustering problems and applied a similar approach.

We observed how the detail level of the monitored API calls can affect the results of clustering and concluded that features should not be based strictly on *apd_level_1* calls, but neither should they contain too much noise. Therefore the best behavioral model was described by API functions from *level 2*. We also compared N-gram choices for N varying from 1 to 9 and observed that a good balance should be chosen between too little behavioral information and too much noise, thus N varying from 5 to 7 yields the best results.

We finally evaluated the resulting clustering models, based on internal metrics as well as external comparison with ground truth and observed that the results are similar to the text clustering problem, when no semantic analysis is performed.

7.1 Possible Improvements and Future Research

Our behavioral model could be refined by selecting only relevant API functions or even adding more which are currently not monitored thus improving the relevance of information gained and possibly achieving better clustering. The system which clusterizes malicious processes could be extended with more clustering algorithms which take advantage of other distances (e.g., Jaccard similarity, Manhattan, etc.) and their results could be checked if it improves our proposed solution.

Future research could be done on applying more ideas from text clustering problems. For example we could perform semantic analysis before building our feature vectors. This way some functions could be identified which are used frequently but bring no extra information (e.g., Sleep) or we can group functions that can be considered synonyms (i.e. they perform the same action, but with different function calls). By doing this each action could be represented uniquely, therefore the features would be more meaningful and better clustering could be achieved.

Acknowledgment. This work was supported by a grant of the Romanian National Authority for Scientific Research and Innovation, CNCS/CCCDI-UEFISCDI, project number PN-III-P2-2.1-PED-2016-2073, within PNCDI III.

References

1. Arthur, D., Vassilvitskii, S.: k-means++: the advantages of careful seeding. In: Proceedings of the Eighteenth Annual ACM-SIAM Symposium on Discrete Algorithms, pp. 1027–1035. Society for Industrial and Applied Mathematics (2007)
2. AV-TEST: Number of malware throughout 2009–2018. https://www.av-test.org/en/statistics/malware/
3. Bayer, U., Comparetti, P.M., Hlauschek, C., Kruegel, C., Kirda, E.: Scalable, behavior-based malware clustering. In: NDSS, vol. 9, pp. 8–11. Citeseer (2009)
4. Bergeron, J., Debbabi, M., Desharnais, J., Erhioui, M.M., Lavoie, Y., Tawbi, N., et al.: Static detection of malicious code in executable programs. Int. J. Req. Eng. **2001**(184–189), 79 (2001)
5. Buchta, C., Kober, M., Feinerer, I., Hornik, K.: Spherical k-means clustering. J. Stat. Softw. **50**(10), 1–22 (2012)
6. Caliński, T., Harabasz, J.: A dendrite method for cluster analysis. Commun. Stat.-Theory Methods **3**(1), 1–27 (1974)
7. Cavnar, W.B., Trenkle, J.M., et al.: N-gram-based text categorization. Ann arbor mi **48113**(2), 161–175 (1994)

8. Davies, D.L., Bouldin, D.W.: A cluster separation measure. IEEE Trans. Pattern Anal. Mach. Intell. **2**, 224–227 (1979)
9. Galkovsky, M.: Dlls the dynamic way. MSDN Library Website (1999)
10. Hassani, M., Seidl, T.: Using internal evaluation measures to validate the quality of diverse stream clustering algorithms. Vietnam J. Comput. Sci. **4**(3), 171–183 (2017)
11. Huang, A.: Similarity measures for text document clustering. In: Proceedings of the Sixth New Zealand Computer Science Research Student Conference (NZCSRSC 2008), Christchurch, New Zealand, pp. 49–56 (2008)
12. Khabia, A., Chandak, M.: A cluster based approach with n-grams at word level for document classification. Int. J. Comput. Appl. **117**(23), 38–42 (2015)
13. Leskovec, J., Rajaraman, A., Ullman, J.D.: Mining of Massive Datasets, pp. 7–15. Cambridge University Press, Cambridge (2014)
14. Li, P., Liu, L., Gao, D., Reiter, M.K.: On challenges in evaluating malware clustering. In: Jha, S., Sommer, R., Kreibich, C. (eds.) RAID 2010. LNCS, vol. 6307, pp. 238–255. Springer, Heidelberg (2010). https://doi.org/10.1007/978-3-642-15512-3_13
15. Malwarebytes: Cybercrime tactics and techniques: Q1 2018. https://www.malwarebytes.com/pdf/white-papers/CTNT-Q1-2018.pdf
16. Perdisci, R., et al.: VAMO: towards a fully automated malware clustering validity analysis. In: Proceedings of the 28th Annual Computer Security Applications Conference, pp. 329–338. ACM (2012)
17. Qiao, Y., He, J., Yang, Y., Ji, L.: Analyzing malware by abstracting the frequent itemsets in API call sequences. In: 2013 12th IEEE International Conference on Trust, Security and Privacy in Computing and Communications, pp. 265–270. IEEE (2013)
18. Ramos, J., et al.: Using TF-IDF to determine word relevance in document queries. In: Proceedings of the First Instructional Conference on Machine Learning, vol. 242, pp. 133–142 (2003)
19. Rieck, K., Trinius, P., Willems, C., Holz, T.: Automatic analysis of malware behavior using machine learning. J. Comput. Secur. **19**(4), 639–668 (2011)
20. Rosenberg, A., Hirschberg, J.: V-measure: a conditional entropy-based external cluster evaluation measure. In: Proceedings of the 2007 Joint Conference on Empirical Methods in Natural Language Processing and Computational Natural Language Learning (EMNLP-CoNLL) (2007)
21. Rousseeuw, P.J.: Silhouettes: a graphical aid to the interpretation and validation of cluster analysis. J. Comput. Appl. Math. **20**, 53–65 (1987)
22. Salton, G., Wong, A., Yang, C.S.: A vector space model for automatic indexing. Commun. ACM **18**(11), 613–620 (1975)
23. Sculley, D.: Web-scale k-means clustering. In: Proceedings of the 19th International Conference on World Wide Web, pp. 1177–1178. ACM (2010)
24. Shankarapani, M.K., Ramamoorthy, S., Movva, R.S., Mukkamala, S.: Malware detection using assembly and API call sequences. J. Comput. Virol. **7**(2), 107–119 (2011)
25. Willems, C., Holz, T., Freiling, F.: Toward automated dynamic malware analysis using cwsandbox. IEEE Secur. Privacy **5**(2), 32–39 (2007)

CloudNet Anti-malware Engine: GPU-Accelerated Network Monitoring for Cloud Services

George Hatzivasilis[1]([✉]), Konstantinos Fysarakis[2],
Ioannis Askoxylakis[1], and Alexander Bilanakos[3]

[1] Institute of Computer Science,
Foundation for Research and Technology – Hellas (FORTH),
N. Plastira 100, 70013 Heraklion, Crete, Greece
hatzivas@ics.forth.gr
[2] Sphynx Technology Solutions, Gubelstr 12, 6300 Zuk, Switzerland
[3] Department of Computer Science, University of Crete,
Voutes University Campus, 70013 Heraklion, Crete, Greece

Abstract. In the modern applications for Internet-of-Things (IoT) and Cyber-Physical Systems (CPSs) heterogeneous embedded devices exchange high volumes of data. Interconnection with cloud services is becoming popular. Thus, enhanced security is imperative but network monitoring is computational intensive. Parallel programming utilizing Graphics Processing Units (GPUs) is a well-tried practice for drastically reducing the computation time in computation intensive domains. This paper presents CloudNet – a lightweight and efficient GPU-accelerated anti-malware engine, utilizing the CUDA General Purpose GPU (GPGPU). The core of the system computes the digests of files using a CUDA-optimized SHA-3 hashing mechanism. Malware digests are stored in a data structure so that detection checks take place as network traffic is processed. Work includes a comparative analysis for three types of data structures (hash table, tree, and array) to identify the most appropriate for this specific field. We develop several versions of two basic variations of applications, including performance comparisons of GPU-accelerated implementation to the reference and optimized CPU implementations. The CloudNet is developed in order to protect CPSs that communicate information to the industrial cloud. A trace of an industrial wind park traffic is utilized for the evaluation of CloudNet, achieving two times faster network monitoring than typical CPU solutions.

Keywords: Cloud · Industrial cloud · Network monitoring ·
Anti-malware · Parallel computing · GPU · CUDA · SHA-3 ·
CPS · IoT · IIoT

1 Introduction

Most users nowadays will not neglect to safeguard their computers and laptops from all types of malicious software. However, the same approach is not always adopted for the devices in the domains of Internet of Things (IoT) and Cyber-Physical Systems (CPSs)

A. P. Fournaris et al. (Eds.): IOSec 2018, LNCS 11398, pp. 122–133, 2019.
https://doi.org/10.1007/978-3-030-12085-6_11

which exchange information with the cloud [1, 2]. Thus, malicious entities can find a new opportunity in attacking these less protected components and infiltrate in the whole network [3]. Drawbacks are mainly occurred due to [3, 4]: (i) poor or non-existent security at the device-end, (ii) poor network segmentation where the devices are directly exposed to the Internet, (iii) unneeded functionality that is left in based on generic development processes, and (iv) the use of the default credentials, which are often hard coded. So, the network monitoring and the inspection of traffic form the device to the cloud is becoming imperative along with the development of new efficient and scalable solutions which can tackle the processing of high volumes of data that are produced by such systems.

A Graphics Processing Unit (GPU) is a specialized electronic circuit designed to process data rapidly on a graphics card. At first, GPUs were deployed for processing images in high volume but later their highly parallel computing capabilities were exploited by a plethora of applications where computing intensive operations had to be performed.

To this effect, NVIDIA [5] offers the Compute Unified Device Architecture (CUDA, [6]) – a parallel computing platform and programming model. Through the use of CUDA, a graphics card can be utilized as a general purpose processing unit; a concept known as General Purpose GPU (GPGPU) computing. Thus, any application can potentially exploit the processing capabilities and highly parallel nature of modern graphics card to achieve significant speed-up factors compared to their CPU-only versions.

Several security sensitive applications require to process data at real-time and in high volumes. Such applications include anti-malware systems that monitor the network traffic or scan the hard disk of a PC to find out malicious data.

In this paper, an efficient and lightweight GPU accelerator for hashing and hash lookup is presented, called CloudNet. The proposed system utilizes an optimized implementation of SHA-3 [7] in GPUs, acting as the core hash function for calculating the digest of examined malwares. Then, we develop and compare several data structures for maintaining the processed data and select the most appropriate of them. We apply the proposed solution in security-related applications for anti-malware detection and real-time malware intrusion detection in network traffic.

The rest paper is organized as follows: Sect. 2 discusses the related studies in the domain. Section 3 presents CloudNet. Section 4 includes the implementation details of the system and provides a comparative analysis of the different reference and optimized implementations of the underlying hash function and the data structures. Finally, Sect. 5 concludes and refers future work.

2   Related Work

The proposed effort is focused in adapting known security solutions in graphics cards. When it comes to applying anti-malware solutions on GPUs, the performance evaluation targets to improve either the general operation of the system or specific inner core elements.

Antivirus engines in GPUs are presented in [8, 9]. GrAVity [8], a massively parallel antivirus engine, modifies ClamAV (an open-source antivirus software, [10]) and exploits the computing power of modern graphic processors to achieve 100 times higher performance than the CPU-only CalmAV. In [9], the authors propose a highly-efficient memory-compression approach for GPU-accelerated virus signature matching. They implement Aho-Corasick and Commentz-Walter automatons for performing GPU-accelerated virus scanning in conjunction with a set of virus signatures from CalmAV. Their antivirus engine is appropriate for real-world software and hardware systems.

Intrusion detection mechanisms for network security that exploit the computation capabilities of GPUs are reported in [11] and [12]. Gnort [11], which is based on the Snort open-source NIDS, is an intrusion detection system that is applied in GPUs to offload the costly pattern matching operation form the CPU. It increases the overall throughput and can be applied either for processing synthetic network traces or monitoring real traffic via an Ethernet interface. In [12], the authors propose a regular expression matching mechanism for intrusion detection on GPUs. Their system achieves a 48 times speedup over traditional CPU implementations.

The main method to create malware signatures is hash functions. To increase the performance of an anti-malware system, one can speed up the process of calculating the digest of the processing data. To take advantage of the parallel computing features in CPUs and, later, GPUs, there was an effort to either create hash functions that can be parallelized or design general mechanisms that can be used to parallelize any hash function. The SHA-3 contest was held to define a new hash function standard. However, Keccak [16], the hash function that won the contest, lacks of an inherent parallel nature. In order to create a parallel implementation that will exploit the potential of GPUs, one has to resort to alternative mechanisms. This can be achieved by introducing a Merkle tree [11] construction; a technique that can be used to parallelize any hash function and the one that was chosen for the presented system as well, as will be detailed later in this work.

CloudNet is a novel anti-malware engine that efficiently utilizes the state-of-the-art SHA-3 function in order to detect malware traffic. It is designed having in mind the intrinsic features and performance requirements of the modern IoT and cloud computing applications (e.g. [13, 14]). The system protects a real industrial setting, where IoT-enabled smart devices and wind turbines exchange information to the industrial cloud [15]. In regards to GrAVity and Gnort, it can be utilized in order to further increase the parallelization of the internal scanning procedure.

3 CloudNet

This implementation involves the development of a lightweight and efficient GPU-accelerated malware identification/hash lookup mechanism based on the SHA-3 [16] hash function. CloudNet exploits the CUDA toolkit and the parallelization capabilities of modern GPUs to improve the performance of the digest computation, i.e. the inner calculations of the chosen cryptographic hash function that will be run on the GPU.

The proposed solution implements two main operations. At the initialization phase, the system takes as input a directory with malware files, computes the digests of each item, and stores them in a data structure. At the processing phase, the system takes network traffic as input, computes the digests of the relevant data segments, and compares them against the information that is maintain in the data structure. Figure 1 illustrates the malware identification phases.

For antimalware engines, computing the hash on an entire file from the start is a waste of resources, whether it's done on CPU or GPU. What you can do instead, is to compute the hash only on a small portion of the file (like the first 2 KB, for instance), then, if it is found in a preliminary hash table, compute the hash value for the rest of the file. For most scanned files, the first hash will not be found (we assume that most files are clean) and the hash computation for the entire file is avoided. Nevertheless, in the rest paper we mention the results for hashing the entire file as the overall setting could be also utilized in other related domains that require full processing, i.e. blockchaining [17].

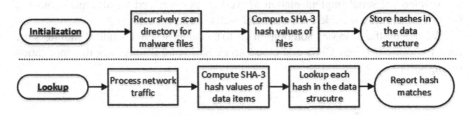

Fig. 1. Functionality sketch of GPU-accelerated mechanism.

The utility could scan the whole hash table looking for matches for the specific hash value it just calculated. This way, it could report back if the specific data exists in the initial hash table and what that item was. Such an identification mechanism could be useful for malware detection on network monitoring or local disks (e.g. to detect malicious or flagged files on the network).

The system maintains a hash-table with the hash values (signatures) of known malwares, which is created during the Initialization phase. Upon execution of the Lookup phase, it computes the digest of input traces using the same hash function and look for matches in the pre-computed values residing on the hash table.

Main operations include:

- Compute a digest
- Compare two digests
- Insert a new digest in the hash table
- Search for a digest in the hash table
- Report malware identification
- Delete or Move detected malicious traffic (optional).

For improving the performance of the GPU accelerated identification and verification solution, we focus on the optimization of the inner digest calculation and the data structure that maintains the processed data. We utilize the CUDA-optimized implementation of SHA-3 [12] to improve the inner operation, where we need to compute the digest of inputted data. In the following, we analyze the performance of different implementations of SHA-3 in CPU and GPU in the different application settings. Moreover, we conduct a comparative analysis along three types of data structures (hash table, binary tree, and array) that can maintain the processed data.

4 Performance Evaluation

This section presents the implementation details of CloudNet. The proposed system was developed and evaluated on a test-bed featuring an Intel Core i7 Processor (6 MB Cache, 2.1 GHz), 8 GB of RAM, an NVIDIA GeForce GTX 1050 GPU (640 cores, 2 GB buffer, 6Gbps memory speed, 1.4 GHz clock) [19], and the Ubuntu 17.10 operating system.

An initial CUDA implementation of the SHA-3 hashing mechanism was compared to the reference serial implementation as well as an optimized serial implementation, both of which are available on the official website [7].

We deploy the proposed solution on an IoT setting, where CloudNet monitors the network traffic between CPSs and cloud services. Figure 2 illustrates the application setting.

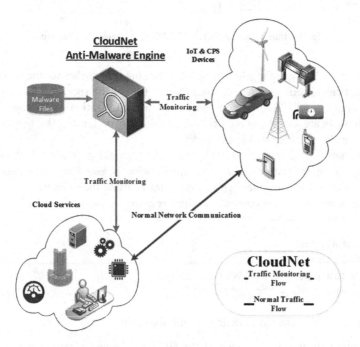

Fig. 2. The CloudNet setting.

As a benchmark, we utilize a trace of a real industrial wind park in Brande, Denmark. The examined Software-Defined Networking (SDN) and Network Function Virtualization (NFV) - enabled wind park is a characteristic use case of the next generation networks operating over 5G communication infrastructures. Several sensing devices and wind turbines transmit data to the backend Supervisory Control and Data Acquisition (SCADA) servers that monitors and/or react to environmental or other operational parameters. The trace focuses on traffic to/from the SCADA servers and was captured for around 1000 s of operation. Totally, more than 20.000 connections with low data rates are included. The TCP connections exhibit 100 ms, 250 ms, and 500 ms end-to-end delay based on the service. The UDP connections have more stringent communication requirements of 10 ms. These numbers are utilized as performance thresholds for the applicability of CloudNet. Figure 3 depicts the Industrial IoT (IIoT) wind park installation.

4.1   Choosing Data Structure

Before proceeding with the GPU implementation, the data structure to be used had to be finalized. To that end, the performance of alternative structures was examined and compared. In specific, array, binary tree, and hash table structures were investigated, focusing on the insertion time (i.e. how long it takes to insert a new entry into the data structure during initialization) and search time (i.e. how long it takes to lookup a specific entry in the data structure). The results of said comparison can be seen in Fig. 4, where it is evident that the hash table has an advantage over alternative structures.

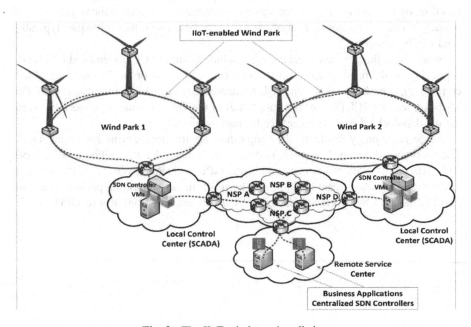

Fig. 3. The IIoT wind part installation.

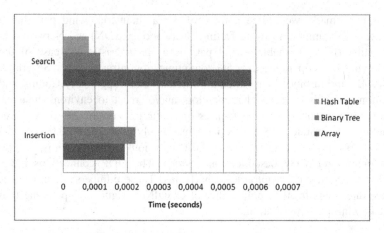

Fig. 4. Data structure performance comparison for CUDA-accelerated implementations.

4.2 GPU Results

Having finalized the data structure to be used, efforts could focus on the development and optimization of the CUDA hashing mechanism.

One way to parallelize any hash function is to look for parallelism in the inner functions, but this is not always an option as hash functions, by nature, are often complex and serialized. The SHA-3 CUDA implementation was based on a technique which can be used to parallelize any hash function, i.e. using a tree hash mode, also known as Merkle tree [20]. With this method, parallelism is realized outside the hash function, by running instances (tree leaves) concurrently and then gathering the results of each instance at an upper level of the tree. More details on the techniques typically used can be found in [21].

In addition, the program checks if the machine features a CUDA-enabled GPU and, depending on the result, then runs the Optimized CPU code or the CUDA code of the cryptographic hash function. On CUDA-enabled devices, the utility also checks the hardware features (CUDA version supported) of the GPU, in order to choose between the overlap-enabled and the basic tree hashing modes.

Some preliminary results of the simple hashing tree mechanism appear in Fig. 5. The results were obtained on a test system featuring an NVIDIA GeForce GTX 1050 GPU [19]. As is evident from the graph, the GPU-accelerated version of the hashing mechanism has a significant advantage in terms of the actual hashing performance, but also suffers extra I/O overhead because of the data transfer from host to GPU.

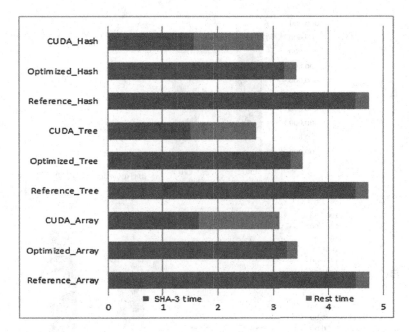

Fig. 5. Comparison of execution and I/O time of SHA-3 implementations.

4.3 Further Optimizations

The execution of the hashing mechanism was successfully improved by exploiting features present on newer generations of GPUs. Overlapping GPU and CPU computations, i.e. having the CPU compute the tree's top node of previous GPU computations, while the GPU processes other kernels, can yield significant improvements. Furthermore, if there is hardware support, data transfers and computations on the GPU can be overlapped as well, yielding further benefits. To accomplish this, page-locked memory and CUDA streams must be used, to allow the succession of transfers and computations in each stream, as described in the CUDA programming guide [18].

In order to assess the performance benefits from using the GPU to speed up the hashing mechanism of the developed application, a test folder was created and was used as a benchmark of the application's execution time. The folder contained 200 relatively small malware files (minimum size 3 MB, maximum size 50 MB, average size 20 MB) and 100 bigger files (minimum size 70 MB, maximum size 170 MB, average size 123 MB) and was used as an input at the application's initialization phase. Therefore the application recursively hashed all files and stored the results in the hash table.

The performance gains from employing the improved GPU implementation, namely overlapping GPU and CPU (top node) computations and the extra performance boost achieved by combining that with GPU transfer and computation overlaps, are evident in Fig. 6A and B. In addition to significantly improving the hashing speed itself, the overlap techniques allowed the minimization of the performance penalties incurred by host-to-GPU and GPU-to-host transfers that are unavoidable in GPU implementations, as can be seen in Fig. 6C.

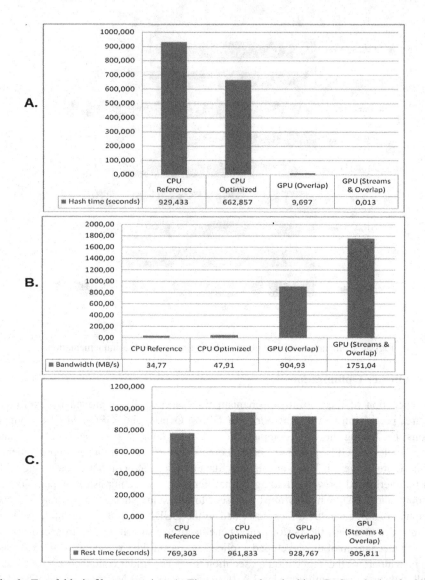

Fig. 6. Test folder's files processing: A. Time consumed on hashing, B. Speed when hashing, and C. Time consumed in non-hashing functions (I/O etc.).

The total execution time of the application when initializing for the given benchmark folder can be seen in Fig. 7. Noticeably, the time consumed on the hashing mechanism itself was successfully minimized by exploiting the GPU, to the point where hashing time is insignificant and the execution time is dominated by input/output and other processes. The latter significantly limits the total speedup achieved in the specific application, as can be seen in Fig. 8A.

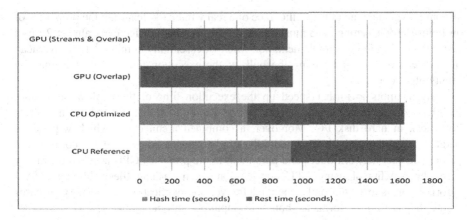

Fig. 7. Total execution time comparison.

Regarding the lookup phase, the GPU implementation's performance is a bit slower than the CPU alternatives, as can be seen in Fig. 8B. This is to be expected as there is the extra overhead of transferring files to and from the GPU. This could be addressed by parallelizing the hash table search, but such an endeavor would only yield noticeable benefits in cases of large tables (i.e. tables storing values of many files). In its current form, the developed application would not benefit in a noticeable way, as the time spent on the lookup phase is not significant compared to other, more time consuming parts of the execution, like the initialization and the hashing itself (especially when run on the CPU).

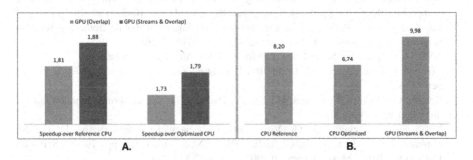

Fig. 8. A. Total speedup and B. Hash lookup times.

5 Conclusion

A lightweight and efficient GPU accelerating hashing and hash lookup mechanism utilizing the CUDA GPGPU toolkit was presented in this paper. We apply the proposed system in an anti-malware intrusion detection application, called CloudNet. Reference and optimized versions in CPU and GPU of the underlying primitives are implemented and a comparative analysis is conducted for selecting the most efficient ones. The system is evaluated under the traffic trace of a real wind park, featuring the properties of an Industrial IoT setting. The most efficient GPU version is effectively almost 2 times faster than the reference implementation in CPU, essentially eliminating the overhead of hash calculations and having the bulk of the execution time being consumed by input/output operations.

Any attempts to further speed up the execution time of the application should, mainly, be focused on the initialization phase, aiming to alleviate the abovementioned bottleneck in hard disk I/O. Moreover, a combined architecture, which will utilize parallel computing in both CPU and GPU can be considered, where CPU cores would process distinct network traces and pass them to the proposed GPU accelerator. In any case, the benefits of using GPU acceleration when hashing files with the SHA-3 algorithm are substantial and beneficial for various applications, especially in cases where they are not performance-bound by input/output operations.

Acknowledgment. This work has received funding from the European Union Horizon's 2020 research and innovation programme under grant agreement No. 780315 (SEMIoTICS). The authors would also like to thank the network engineers maintaining the subject wind park in Brande, Denmark for their valuable input in interpreting the network traces.

References

1. Zhu, C., Shu, L., Leung, V.C.M., Guo, S., Zhang, Y., Yang, L.T.: Secure multimedia big data in trust-assisted sensor-cloud for smart city. IEEE Commun. Mag. **55**(12), 24–30 (2017)
2. Zhu, C., Zhou, H., Leung, V.C.M., Wang, K., Zhang, Y., Yang, L.T.: Toward big data in green city. IEEE Commun. Mag. **55**(11), 14–18 (2017)
3. Antonakakis, M., et al.: Understanding the Mirai Botnet. In: 26th Usenix Security Symposium (SS), 16–18 August, Vancouver, BC, Canada, pp. 1093–1110 (2017)
4. Lu, Z., Wang, W., Wang, C.: On the evolution and impact of mobile Botnets in wireless networks. IEEE Trans. Mob. Comput. **15**(9), 2304–2316 (2016)
5. NVIDIA Corporation, Santa Clara, California, USA. http://www.nvidia.com/
6. Compute Unified Device Architecture (CUDA). http://www.nvidia.com/object/cuda_home_new.html
7. Bertoni, G., Daemen, J., Peeters, M., Van Assche, G.: The Keccak sponge function family. http://keccak.noekeon.org/
8. Vasiliadis, G., Ioannidis, S.: GrAVity: a massively parallel antivirus engine. In: Jha, S., Sommer, R., Kreibich, C. (eds.) RAID 2010. LNCS, vol. 6307, pp. 79–96. Springer, Heidelberg (2010). https://doi.org/10.1007/978-3-642-15512-3_5
9. Pungila, C., Negru, V.: A highly-efficient memory-compression approach for GPU-accelerated virus signature matching. In: Gollmann, D., Freiling, F.C. (eds.) ISC 2012. LNCS, vol. 7483, pp. 354–369. Springer, Heidelberg (2012). https://doi.org/10.1007/978-3-642-33383-5_22
10. Clam AntiVirus, Open Source (GPL) antivirus engine. http://www.clamav.net
11. Vasiliadis, G., Antonatos, S., Polychronakis, M., Markatos, E.P., Ioannidis, S.: Gnort: high performance network intrusion detection using graphics processors. In: Lippmann, R., Kirda, E., Trachtenberg, A. (eds.) RAID 2008. LNCS, vol. 5230, pp. 116–134. Springer, Heidelberg (2008). https://doi.org/10.1007/978-3-540-87403-4_7

12. Vasiliadis, G., Polychronakis, M., Antonatos, S., Markatos, E.P., Ioannidis, S.: Regular expression matching on graphics hardware for intrusion detection. In: Kirda, E., Jha, S., Balzarotti, D. (eds.) RAID 2009. LNCS, vol. 5758, pp. 265–283. Springer, Heidelberg (2009). https://doi.org/10.1007/978-3-642-04342-0_14
13. Hatzivasilis, G., Papaefstathiou, I., Manifavas, C.: SCOTRES: secure routing for IoT and CPS. IEEE Internet Things J. (IoT) 4(6), 2129–2141 (2017)
14. Hatzivasilis, G., Papaefstathiou, I., Manifavas, C.: Real-time management of railway CPS. In: 5th EUROMICRO/IEEE Workshop on Embedded and Cyber-Physical Systems, ECYPS 2017, 11–15 June, Bar, Montenegro. IEEE (2017)
15. Hatzivasilis, G., Fysarakis, K., Soultatos, O., Askoxylakis, I., Papaefstathiou, I., Demetriou, G.: The industrial internet of things as an enabler for a circular economy Hy-LP: a novel IIoT protocol, evaluated on a Wind Park's SDN/NFV-enabled 5G industrial network. Comput. Commun. Spec. Issue Energy-aware Des. Sustain. 5G Netw. 119, 127–137 (2018)
16. National Institute of Standards & Technology (NIST): SHA-3 Winner Announcement. http://csrc.nist.gov/groups/ST/hash/sha-3/winner_sha-3.html
17. Alexandris, G., Alexaki, S., Katos, V., Hatzivasilis, G.: Blockchains as enablers for auditing cooperative circular economy networks. In: 23rd IEEE International Workshop on Computer Aided Modeling and Design of Communication Links and Networks, CAMAD 2018, 17–19 September, Barcelona, Spain, pp. 1–7. IEEE (2018)
18. NVIDIA Jetson TK1. http://www.nvidia.com/object/jetson-tk1-embedded-dev-kit.html
19. NVIDIA: GeForce GTX 1050. https://www.nvidia.com/en-us/geforce/products/10series/geforce-gtx-1050/
20. Merkle, R.C.: A certified digital signature. In: Brassard, G. (ed.) CRYPTO 1989. LNCS, vol. 435, pp. 218–238. Springer, New York (1990). https://doi.org/10.1007/0-387-34805-0_21
21. Sevestre, G.: Keccak tree hashing on GPU, using NVIDIA CUDA API. https://sites.google.com/site/keccaktreegpu/

Full Content Search in Malware Collections

Andrei Mihalca[1,2(✉)] and Ciprian Oprişa[1,2]

[1] Bitdefender, 1, Cuza Vodă Street, City Business Center,
400107 Cluj-Napoca, Romania
mihalca.andrei.vasile@gmail.com, coprisa@bitdefender.com
[2] Technical University of Cluj-Napoca, 28, Gh. Bariţiu Street, room M03,
400027 Cluj-Napoca, Romania

Abstract. This paper aims to provide the techniques for performing fast searches by content in large malware collections. The ability to retrieve malware samples sharing a given content is important for malware researchers that look for previous instances of a new sample or test new signatures. We propose a data structure that allows fast searches and can be continuously expanded with new samples. The performance and the scalability of our solution are proved through experiments on real-world malware.

Keywords: Malware · Big data · Content search

1 Introduction

Recent studies show that malware is still a major threat to computer systems, as there are currently 780 millions distinct malware samples, their numbers growing by millions each month [4]. A more detailed description of the malware ecosystem is present in [5], where the concepts of malware families and malware variants are described. The millions of malware samples that are active on the market in a given time frame belong to a much lower number of malware families, although they represent distinct pieces of software.

Malware authors employ obfuscation techniques and packers in order to produce multiple malware binaries that will not be detected by a regular anti-virus signature. After the current group of samples currently released (named a *variant*) is detected by most anti-virus engines, the authors will change the obfuscation approach and release a new variant, the binary content being different enough from the previous one to evade detection.

To detect morphing threats, anti-virus researchers will search for common features among samples belonging to the same malware variant. Identifying these samples is a difficult problem, given the size of the malware corpus. Human researchers and automata can benefit from a search system able to retrieve existing samples based on their content.

A. P. Fournaris et al. (Eds.): IOSec 2018, LNCS 11398, pp. 134–145, 2019.
https://doi.org/10.1007/978-3-030-12085-6_12

This paper aims to provide the techniques for performing such searches very fast, while being able to update the existing collection with new samples every day. Our approach is based on the *inverted index* data structure, that associate each fixed-length sequence of bytes with a list of files that contain it. By employing this data structure, we avoid the naive algorithm that searches for the given sequence of bytes in every file from the collection. However, such a data structure is more difficult to maintain, our experiments showing that general purpose database management system fail to achieve the desired performance.

The following section lists similar research, emphasizing the differences from our approach. The third section presents the principles for building and maintaining the index data structure, while the fourth one argues why n-grams extracted from binary files can be considered big data. The experimental results focus on the performance of our algorithms. The paper ends with the conclusions section.

2   Related Work

A similar approach, proposed by Wesley Jin et al., exposed the idea of building a collection of offset-free unique n-grams generated from a binary file, using 1-byte sliding [7]. Initially, they tried to build inverted index using open-source technologies, such as PostgreSQL [6], MongoDB [12], Tokyo Cabinet [10] or Redis [11].

There were two attempts for creating the inverted index using PostgreSQL. First approach did not offer desired insertion performance. In this case, a set of 3,465 malware files could not be processed within a week. In the second approach, they redesigned the database, that resulted in a better insert performance, but the disk usage was unacceptable.

Then, they tried to create the inverted index using Tokyo Cabinet and MongoDB, which are NoSQL style open-source databases. Both technologies provide attractive features, such as fast lists updates, but the progress of indexing the data from 3,465 files, was less than 50% after two days of processing. Another existing tehnology, Redis, which is an in-memory key-value store, that can be used as a database or as a cache, provided faster data fetching and updating, but the limit of key space (maximum 2^{32} keys), proved is infeasible for storing the inverted index.

Thus, they was decided to build the inverted index from scratch. The inverted index architecture had two major components: the n-grams list and the postings list. The n-grams list was a sequence of 64-bit offsets into the postings lists. The offset for a n-gram was located by taking its $n-1$ most significant bytes, shifting them by one byte to the right, and multiplying the result by 8. Each posting list entry consisted of the following fields: n-gram (4 bytes), compression type along with compressed data size (4 bytes) and compressed list of file identifiers. Then, they had the idea of creating separate indexes for batches of files in memory, and flushing them to disk. The algorithm for the index construction had three logical parts:

1. Extraction of unique n-grams from all the files in a batch using 1-sliding;

2. Common n-grams across all of the files are merged into a single unified list, using a Loser Tree;
3. File identifiers for each n-gram are compressed to form posting entries.

Overall complexity for this algorithm resulted in $O(M \cdot N + N \cdot \log_2(N))$, where M is the number of files in a batch and N is average file size.

In the article [13] n-grams were used for executable code similarity, in order to detect malware. Here was presented the idea of marking library code as invalid, through his representative n-grams, for increasing malware detection algorithm precision. This approach can be applied in the current context for marking too frequent n-grams as invalid, with the benefit of reducing the posting lists average size.

3   Index Principles

3.1   The Naive Approach

Before presenting our solution we will first discuss the naive approach and highlight its drawbacks. Given a large files collection, we need to search for a given sequence of bytes and output the list of all the files that contain it. The naive solution would be to simply store the entire collection on a single server or on a distributed system and perform each search sequentially.

For instance, if we had 1000 files, with an average size of 100 KB each, our collection would take about 100 MB. The sequential search for the given content in the entire collection can be performed using a simple approach like the `memmem` function [2], or using more advanced algorithms like Rabin-Karp [9] or Aho-Corasick [3]. Either way, the running time for the search will be given by the time necessary to read the data from the disk. On a disk with a reading speed of 100 MB/s, the entire search would take about a second.

On the other hand, if we increase the number of files to 1 million (which is more realistic for a malware collection), the search time would linearly increase to 1000 s, which is not acceptable in practical situations. In the rest of this section we will present an approach based on n-grams and inverted index that offers a search time that doesn't grow linearly with the collection size.

3.2   Binary Files Representation as n-grams

The terms used in the inverted index are defined as n-grams, which are sequences of n bytes, got from a sliding window of n bytes, window that is shifted with a single position, through the file's data (Fig. 1). This implies that the minimum size of file that is going to be indexed is n bytes. The maximum number of n-grams that can be extracted from a binary file is $s - n + 1$, where s is the size of the file in bytes. The n-grams are extracted uniquely, because we propose an offset-free indexing solution. In order to extract the n-grams uniquely, several data structures and algorithms can be used:

1. A bitmap, if $n \leq 4$. In the worst case, 2^{32} bits are necessary for keeping the n-ngrams uniquely. This can be achieved by using an array of 512 MB. Thus, the complexity for extracting unique n-grams from a file of size s is $O(s)$.
2. Otherwise, if $n > 4$, a map data structure can be used, which provides a $O(s \cdot \log_2(s))$ complexity for n-gram extraction.
3. Another option is using of a sorted array of s elements, each having the size n, where the duplicate elements are removed. This results in a time complexity of $O(s \cdot \log_2(s))$.

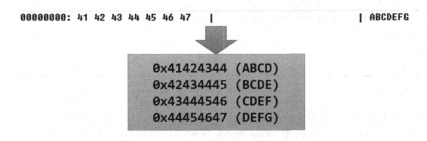

Fig. 1. The process of n-gram extraction

Some n-grams don't provide useful information. In most of the cases, those correspond to sequences of bytes present in every file having a specific format. For example, all PDF documents have the n-gram of 4 bytes 0x25504446 (corresponds to the string "%PDF"). This category of n-grams must be filtered [13], in order to prevent the occurrence of huge posting lists. Also, by filtering those n-grams, the total size of the inverted index decreases.

A naive approach for filtering the n-grams implies the establishment of a threshold for a n-gram's appearances within a malware collection. If the count of appearances exceeds that threshold, the n-gram is marked as invalid.

Another approach for invalidating n-grams is an adaptation of the inverse document frequency statistic [8]. We define a document as the set of n-grams which belongs to a specific file format. Inverse document frequency measure (idf) is defined as:

$$idf(t, D) = log \frac{N}{1 + |t \in D : t \in d|} \tag{1}$$

where D is the set of all n-grams in collection, and N is the number of distinct file formats in collection. $|t \in D : t \in d|$ represents the number of file formats that have n-gram t.

In order to store the invalid n-grams, we propose two data structures: a bitmap, or a sorted array. When the count of invalid n-grams is lower than 1000, the sorted array should be used. Otherwise, the bitmap represents the better option. When the sorted array is used, for a total of M invalid n-grams, the time complexity for checking if a n-gram is valid, is $O(M)$. On the other hand, when the bitmap is used, the same operation takes $O(1)$ time complexity.

Algorithm 1. Aglorithm for n-gram extraction

Input : path P to binary file and its size s
Output: set of valid n-grams from the file
1 Content $\leftarrow$ ReadFile(P)
2 Ngrams $\leftarrow \emptyset$
3 InvalidNgrams $\leftarrow$ LoadInvalidNgrams()
4 NgramBitmap $\leftarrow$ CreateNewBitmap(2^{32})
5 **for** $i \leftarrow 0$ **to** $s - 4$ **do**
6 | N $\leftarrow$ GetNgram(Content, i)
7 | **if** $\neg$ *IsBitSet(NgramBitmap, N)* $\wedge \neg$ *IsBitSet(InvalidNgrams, N)* **then**
8 | | Ngrams $\leftarrow$ Ngrams $\cup \{$N$\}$
9 | | SetBit(NgramBitmap, N)
10 | **end**
11 **end**
12 **return** *Ngrams*

The Algorithm 1, for extracting the n-grams from a file with size s, when $n = 4$, is described forwards. The procedure *ReadFile(P)* reads the content of the file identified by path P. Then, *LoadInvalidNgrams* is used for loading the invalid n-grams bitmap. Also, the procedure *CreateNewBitmap(B)* creates a new bitmap having B bits. *GetNgram(Buffer, Offset)* is used for getting a n-gram from a offset within a buffer. Then, the procedures *IsBitSet(Bitmap, BitIndex)*, and *SetBit(Bitmap, BitIndex)*, are used for checking if a bit is set, and for setting a bit, respectively, within a bitmap. The time complexity for the algorithm is $O(s)$.

3.3   The Inverted Index

When searching for binary content in malware collections, the naive approach can be used. This implies searching each file's data for a given sequence of bytes. Given the length of a sequence m, and the size of a file s, we have the time complexity of $O(m \cdot s)$ for searching the sequence within that file. For example, having a sequence of 16 bytes to be searched within a collection that has one million files with the average size of 1 MB, and an average reading speed of the disk of 100 MB/s (which results in the capability of scanning approximately an average of 80 files per second), we can search that sequence in 3 h and a half.

The inverted index proposed in this paper is similar to the one created by Jin et al. [7], having also a table with references to the posting lists. We propose the usage of a variable length reference, despite of 8 bytes fixed length in [7]. Also, our solution was designed for the maximum performance of full content indexing given a n-gram having a length of **4 bytes** ($n = 4$). This value offered the best ratio between the postings lists size and the reference table size. Within a set of 100,000 files with random file formats, we found 99.93% ($4.29 \cdot 10^9$ unique 4 byte n-grams) of n-grams with length 4 bytes. On the same set, we found $2.35 \cdot 10^{-7}$% ($43.6 \cdot 10^9$ unique 8 byte n-grams) of n-grams with length 8 bytes. Although the posting lists average size is reasonable when choosing the n-gram size of 8 bytes, the references table is too difficult to be managed.

identifier count (4B)	list of identifiers

Fig. 2. Posting lists format

As mentioned above, within reference table, the entries can have variable length. When the size of 4 bytes is used for n-gram, the maximum reference count is 2^{32}. The posting lists will have the format shown in Fig. 2, where each file identifier takes also 4 bytes. This implies that the posting lists total size, or posting lists offsets, are multiples of 4 bytes, which makes possible to reference X bytes of data using $X/4$ positions. Having Y positions, lets define the number of necessary bits for representing $Y - 1$ (the last position) as $Z = \lfloor log2Y \rfloor$. The formula for computing the size of a reference is $RefSize = Z/8$, if Z is multiple of 8, and $RefSize = Z/8 + 1$ otherwise.

In order to store the reference table to disk, two formats can be used, as is shown in Fig. 3. The first approach is to store a table having 2^{32} entries, each of $RefSize$ bytes, to disk, that results in $O(1)$ time complexity for getting a n-gram's posting list. The other one, implies the storing of sorted pairs $<$**n-gram, reference**$>$, by n-gram, for each n-gram that has a posting list associated. This approach provides the $O(\log_2 M)$ time complexity, where M is the count of the unique n-grams that appear in collection. To determine the format that should be used, we compare the total size of the full reference table, $2^{32} \cdot RefSize$, to the total size of the $<$**n-gram, reference**$>$ pairs, given by $(4 + RefCount) \cdot M$.

reference #0
reference #1
reference #2
...
reference #2^{32}-1

n-gram #0	reference #0
n-gram #1	reference #1
n-gram #2	reference #2
...	...
n-gram #M-1	reference #M-1

(a) Full reference table   (b) Paired reference table

Fig. 3. Reference table formats

The inverted index should be composed by several partial indexes, which can be built using a configurable amount of files. This results in fast removal of older indexed data. The posting lists must be kept uniquely. Running a brief test, using only 321 binary files, we found 19,117,531 posting lists, of which 959,565 (5.015%) were unique. In order to keep the posting lists unique, a hashtable can be used. It is recommended to use a hash function that has a result size of 4 bytes, such as CRC-32 [1]. In this case, within the hashtable, for each CRC-32 on a posting list's data, a reference to that posting list, or a list of references to other posting lists, with the same CRC-32, can be associated. To set, or to retrieve, a posting list's reference, the $O(1)$ time complexity is achieved.

4 Binary n-grams as Big Data

The construction of the inverted index takes a huge amount of time using off-the-shelf technologies, like Redis, Mongo DB or PostgreSQL [7]. In order to provide a reasonable performance for building the inverted index, we developed a custom solution. When indexing a binary file, the following operations are necessary:

- the n-gram extraction, which, in most of the cases, is reasonably fast;
- fetching of the existing posting lists for extracted n-grams;
- the update of the posting lists;
- updating the reference table entries.

For example, given a file of 1 MB, there will be about 3 million operations that have to be made, after the n-grams were extracted. Common data indexing structures, such as B+ trees, or red-black trees, offer, among the best cases, the time complexity of $O(\log_2 N)$. To store those data structures, a huge amount of main memory is necessary: for each key, two memory references are necessary, which, on a 64-bit system, occupy 16 bytes.

We talk about Big Data in the context of binary n-grams because of the following reasons:

- within a collection of M binary files, $2^M - 1$ distinct posting lists can be necessary;
- for each MB of data, 3 million operations have to be performed to index that data;
- usually, the automated malware detection systems, process more than 500,000 samples a day, with an average size of 900 KB.

Given the amount of operations necessary for indexing a single file, we build the partial indexes into the main memory, and finally, we flush them to disk. The inverted index presented in [7] was built using a single threaded approach. According to the presumptive huge number of operations, for indexing a single binary file, our approach uses parallelism for improved performance. The Algorithm 2 for adding the n-grams of a binary file to the inverted index is straight-forward: for each n-gram extracted, add the identifier of the file to its posting list. To extract the n-grams from the binary files, several threads can be used. Each thread should take the path to a file from a queue, and get its n-grams. When $n = 4$, each thread needs 512 MB of main memory for the bitmap that is used for the extracted n-grams uniqueness. The bitmap that stores the invalid n-grams should be shared by all threads.

Although the n-gram extraction process was improved considerably, the process of updating the posting lists associated to the n-grams is still difficult to improve, because of the exclusive access needed for writing the data structures. We used the following data structures for building the inverted index, when $n = 4$:

- an array of 2^{32} entries, each entry having 4 bytes. The indices of this array correspond to n-grams, and the entries correspond to its posting list reference identifier;
- a table of references, to store the references to the posting lists. This table increases as new posting lists are created. The indices of this table are the entries of the array above;
- an array of 2^{32} entries, of 4 bytes each, used to keep the association between a hash value (CRC-32) on a posting list's data, and it's reference identifier, or a list of reference identifiers that have the same hash value. This array ensures the uniqueness of the posting lists;

Algorithm 2. Algorithm for associating a file identifier to a n-gram

Input : a n-gram N and a file identifier F
1 ExistingPostingList ← GetPostingList(N)
2 **if** $ExistingPostingList = \emptyset$ **then**
3 | NewPostingList ← {F}
4 **else**
5 | NewPostingList ← {F} ∪ ExistingPostingList
6 **end**
7 HashValue ← HashFunction(NewPostingList)
8 PostingListId ← GetPostingListId(HashValue)
9 **if** $PostingListId = NULL$ **then**
10 | PostingListId ← AddNewPostingList(HashValue, NewPostingList)
11 **end**
12 SetPostingListId(N, PostingListId)

In the Algorithm 2, the procedure *GetPostingList(Ngram)* is used for retrieving the posting list of a n-gram. Then *HashFunction(Data)* denotes a generic hashing function applied on a buffer of data. Also, *GetPostingListId(HashValue)* is used to get the reference identifier for a hash value. Finally, the procedures *AddNewPostingList(HashValue, NewPostingList)*, and *SetPostingListId(Ngram, PostingListId)*, are used to associate a hash value to a new posting list, and to associate a posting list reference identifier to a n-gram, respectively. The time complexity of the Algorithm 2 is $O(K)$, where K is the maximum length of a posting list. Thus, the time complexity to index the data of a file having the size s is $O(s \cdot K)$. Least but not last, when the posting lists are written to disk, the references to the main memory locations are replaced with the offsets to the file on disk.

5 Experimental Results

In order to evaluate the performance of building inverted index, several sets of
binary files, with random format, having sizes from 1,000 to 30,000, were taken.
We used the naive approach for n-gram invalidation, for maximum performance
of index building algorithm. Also, maximum number of bytes that are indexed
from a binary file, was limited to 32 MB. The performance of index building is
shown in Fig. 4. Although the complexity for algorithm is, in this case, $O(N \cdot K)$,
the blue graph from Fig. 4 can be associated to a square function. This was a
consequence of using a variable sized reference table described above. When there
is no entry left to store a posting list reference, the table is being reallocated,
its size increasing by X empty slots. The solution for fixing the performance
problems appeared, was increasing X. Thus, the red graph from Fig. 4 shows a
linear characteristic for building of inverted index. Performance for flushing the
partial index to disk, settles under 312 s, no matter how many files were indexed.
Figure 5a shows that this depends mostly on the disk load at a time. Also, it
can be seen a drop of performance regarding index flushing somewhere between
8,000 and 9,000 files. This is the point when full reference table is used instead
of paired reference table.

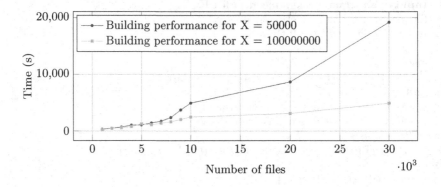

Fig. 4. Index building performance (Color figure online)

Performance for n-gram fetching is also related to the size of posting lists. If
posting lists size is limited to K, then the complexity for fetching file identifiers
for a list of n-grams having N elements is $O(K \cdot N)$. Otherwise, if posting lists
size is not limited, the same operations have a $O(M \cdot N)$ complexity. Within
current design, the posting lists size was limited by the naive approach used for
n-gram invalidation. Thus, the graph shown in Fig. 5b can be approximated to
a linear function. For getting the files where a sequence of 49,900 bytes appears,
5.302 s were necessary, which is significantly better than the naive approach for
searching sequences within malware collections.

Figure 6 shows that for small batches, under 10,000 files, the index size is
double to the size of the batch. As the total batch size increases to 30,000 files,

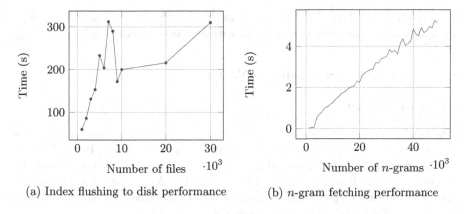

(a) Index flushing to disk performance   (b) n-gram fetching performance

Fig. 5. Index flushing and n-gram fetching performance

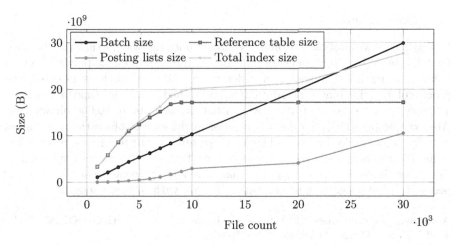

Fig. 6. Disk usage stats

the index size tends to be less than the batch size. This is the reason why a larger amount of binary files have to be indexed at a time.

When it comes to the scalability of the solution, we propose the building of several partial inverted indexes on distinct machines, in parallel. Afterwards, those indexes can be merged.

We ran a test on a collection of 978,668 binary files. It took 57 h of processing in order to index the data of this collection, using a single machine, and 65 GB of main memory. Each partial inverted index that we have built had data from at most 25,000 files. The number of the resulted partial indexes from this collection of files was 50. The average time for indexing a single file's data was 0.211 s. The total size on disk for the collection was 817 GB, and the size on disk for all the partial indexes was 1116 GB, which meant a 1.36 out/in ratio. This result demonstrates the capability of our solution to index 412,000 binary files a day, using a single machine. If there are more binary files to be indexed within a single day, more machines can be used, without performance penalties.

6   Conclusions and Future Work

6.1   Future Work

A form of index compression should be developed, in order to reduce index size on disk. Also, new ways of invalidating n-grams can be proposed. Parallelism for n-gram insertion can be increased as well, by using distinct tables to keep the n-gram to posting lists association. This means that the n-grams must be sorted when they are extracted from the binary file. Parallelization must be used as well for searching files that have a sequence of n-grams.

6.2   Conclusions

In this paper we proposed a binary content indexing system that can be used for full content search in malware collections. The system builds partial inverted indexes, using RAM memory, in order to improve, as much as possible, the process of inserting binary files data. It was obtained an average time for inserting a binary file's n-grams of 0.202 s, within batches of 1,000 to 30,000 binary files. Also, the proposed solution passes, in most of the cases, obfuscation techniques used by malware, by indexing their memory dumps. For fetching a posting list of file identifiers, associated to a n-gram, constant search time was obtained. If the system is used for searching files that have a given sequence of n-grams, the necessary time for getting results varies linearly with sequence length.

Acknowledgment. Research supported, in part, by EC H2020 SMESEC GA #740787 and EC H2020 CIPSEC GA #700378.

References

1. 32-bit CRC algorithm (2018). https://msdn.microsoft.com/en-us/library/dd905031.aspx
2. Linux programmer's manual (2018). http://man7.org/linux/man-pages/man3/memmem.3.html
3. Aho, A.V., Corasick, M.J.: Efficient string matching: an aid to bibliographic search. Commun. ACM **18**(6), 333–340 (1975)
4. AV-Test: Malware statistics (2017). http://www.av-test.org/en/statistics/malware/
5. Chen, Z., Roussopoulos, M., Liang, Z., Zhang, Y., Chen, Z., Delis, A.: Malware characteristics and threats on the internet ecosystem. J. Syst. Softw. **85**(7), 1650–1672 (2012)
6. The PostgreSQL Global Development Group: PostgreSQL (2018). https://www.postgresql.org/

7. Jin, W., Hines, C., Cohen, C., Narasimhan, P.: A scalable search index for binary files. In: Proceedings of the 2012 7th International Conference on Malicious and Unwanted Software (MALWARE), MALWARE 2012, pp. 94–103. IEEE Computer Society, Washington, DC, USA (2012). http://dx.doi.org/10.1109/MALWARE.2012.6461014

8. Jurafsky, D., Martin, J.H.: Speech and Language Processing: An Introduction to Natural Language Processing, Computational Linguistics, and Speech Recognition, 1st edn. Prentice Hall PTR, Upper Saddle River (2000)

9. Karp, R.M., Rabin, M.O.: Efficient randomized pattern-matching algorithms. IBM J. Res. Dev. **31**(2), 249–260 (1987)

10. FAL Labs: Tokyocabinet (2018). http://fallabs.com/tokyocabinet/

11. Redis Labs: Redis (2018). https://redis.io/

12. MongoDB, Inc: MongoDB (2018). https://www.mongodb.com/

13. Oprisa, C., Cabau, G., Colesa, A.: From plagiarism to malware detection. In: 2013 15th International Symposium on Symbolic and Numeric Algorithms for Scientific Computing, pp. 227–234, September 2013

Author Index

Printed in the United States
By Bookmasters